BEYOND BITCOIN INVESTING

Why other cryptocurrencies are so important and easy to make digital cash now

Sweet Smart Books

accurate, up to date, reliable, complete information. No warranties of any kind are declared or implied. Readers acknowledge that the author is not engaged in the rendering of legal, financial, medical or professional advice. The content within this book has been derived from various sources. Please consult a licensed professional before attempting any techniques outlined in this book.

By reading this document, the reader agrees that under no circumstances is the author responsible for any losses, direct or indirect, that are incurred as a result of the use of the information contained within this document, including, but not limited to, errors, omissions, or inaccuracies.

Table of Contents

Introduction

Investment is a way to increase your savings by buying an asset for a particular time frame. The financial world has a lot of financial instruments that an individual can invest in. Choosing where to invest is an entirely individual preference, and it will always be that way. This book explains different cryptocurrency coins that are now in demand and can give you high returns over the years.

To understand Bitcoin and other alternative cryptocurrencies from a financial perspective, you need to first have some knowledge of different financial instruments that are available to investors. Understanding alternatives and how they function is an extremely important skill for an investor.

What is a Financial Instrument?

A financial instrument is a legal document that can be traded individually or collectively to another trader whenever the original contract owner wants. There are different types of financial instruments that a person needs to be aware of before starting their career in investing.

Stocks

Stocks are the most popular of all financial instruments. When you buy a stock, you are purchasing a small portion of a company. All publicly traded companies contribute to economic growth and can thus change the economy over the years.

For example, during the 1990s, there was a huge Internet boom, and all stocks related to Internet technologies were flying high. This encouraged more startups, and it completely changed how the world works. Despite the bust that followed, over 20 years later, we are now completely dependent on the Internet and its services.

Stocks directly affect a country's economy. As a financial instrument, stocks are both versatile and complex. You need to be extremely knowledgeable to make money on the stock market. For a beginner, long-term investing in growth stocks is the preferred way to get into stock markets. The only downside of the stock market is that it is volatile, and many factors drive price change. It is best to be extremely careful about economic policies, politics, and the psychological factors that influence investors when you become a stock trader or investor.

Mutual Funds

Mutual funds are for individuals who are not as technically or fundamentally aware of where to invest their money in the stock market. A mutual fund collects a pool of money from thousands of investors and invests that pool in different stocks in various sectors and sub-sectors.

Talented stock investors will control where your money should go according to their calculations and observations. The only problem with mutual funds is you cannot make profits when the market is down.

To counter this problem, hedge funds have emerged and provide a definite rise in your investment. However, hedge funds are only available for rich investors with millions, whereas mutual funds are accessible to retail investors.

Bank Fixed Deposits

Fixed deposits are straightforward. All you need to do is deposit a sum of money into your bank account, and you will get a percentage as interest every year for that sum of money. Fixed deposits are easy to get into but provide very little profit in the long term. However, a lot of people prefer fixed deposits because there is little risk in using them.

Real Estate

Real estate is an entirely different investment choice. It is best to have a good network and be able to correctly estimate whether land and housing prices will rise depending on local factors. Real estate is fieldwork and is risky if you make a wrong judgment over a change in prices.

It is also very difficult to find a seller who will sell a property for the amount you want. It also involves a lot of intermediaries that lower your share of the profit. Despite these flaws, real estate is still a reliable way to increase your money.

Gold

Gold is a classic investment. The price of gold has increased over the years, and with the current economic factors, it is still a good choice of investment. Gold can be used to get loans from banks or other individuals quickly. People are now also buying digital gold.

Business

Starting a business is also an investment choice. However, unlike all the others mentioned above, this is the toughest one. Starting a business needs capital, space, vision, and a clear set of goals.

For example, if you want to start a restaurant, you need to select a space, buy furniture, hire a cook and other staff, and set up a website or social media page to attract visitors. A business can go wrong even with a lot of hard work. It is also difficult to close a business and liquidate all your investment in it.

Despite all these reasons, small businesses are booming worldwide, and there is a high chance of success in it if you make the right choices.

Derivatives

Derivatives are financial instruments such as stocks, bonds, futures, and forwards. A lot of investors are now using derivatives to bet on the performance of the underlying asset. To understand derivatives, you need first to understand stocks and their performance. Derivatives are legal agreements that will expire after some time. They are like insurance contracts but with a lot of risks.

Cryptocurrency

The difference between the aforementioned financial instruments and cryptocurrency is that cryptocurrency is decentralized. When you buy stocks or options, there will be a centralized institution that controls these financial instruments. These centralized institutions, such as banks, hold the monopoly power to decide what to do with your money.

When the housing bubble burst, many real estate owners lost a lot of money. People lost jobs, unemployment peaked, and a lot of individuals lost their savings. The world suffered, but the banks responsible for this were supported by the government. Even though they were held accountable, they still bounced back, unlike everyday people who lost a lot during this crisis.

Centralization and monopoly help only a few people when a crisis occurs, regardless of the problem. There is no denying that when Bitcoin was announced during this crisis in 2008, there was overwhelming enthusiasm from investors. It changed how the world treats currency and is poised to revolutionize many other platforms with cryptocurrency.

Investing in cryptocurrency is investing in the future. Over more than a decade, Bitcoin has risen from a few cents to approximately $50,000 a coin now. Cryptocurrency is currently a perfect investment to gain huge profits and stop being controlled by centralized institutions.

We will be talking about different advantages and strategies an investor can use in cryptocurrency throughout this book.

What Are You Going to Learn in This Book?

This book is a comprehensive introduction for an investor to understand the importance of investing in cryptocurrency. Our main focus will be explaining to the readers about blockchain, Bitcoin, and other cryptocurrencies that have the same potential as Bitcoin.

If you are a beginner in the cryptocurrency world, we suggest you read each chapter in order. If you only want to know more about alternatives to Bitcoin, then it is better if you start reading from Chapter 4.

How to Use This Book

This is a beginner's book that quickly explains complex topics. We use various techniques to present the ideas in this book so they can be easily understood by everyone. To completely grasp the concept of this book, we suggest you use the following methods:

1. Take notes while reading. Make mind maps using mind-mapping software to easily review the important snippets that are present.

2. Use cognitive learning techniques to understand the concepts explained. You can also teach someone with no knowledge of these concepts to reinforce what you have learned.

Many books on the market explain these topics, but you have chosen our book to help you understand the importance of alternative coins for investing. We will try our best to help you understand these complex topics so you can invest with confidence.

Chapter 1: Bitcoin for Dummies

Bitcoin popularized the concept of blockchain. After ten years, there are hundreds of independent and isolated blockchains similar to Bitcoin running in hundreds of thousands of computers worldwide. While the fundamental principle of the blockchain remains, the same, different cryptocurrencies are introducing interesting and revolutionizing concepts within the domain. This chapter is for readers who are unaware of the idea of blockchain and Bitcoin with an excellent explanation.

What Is a Blockchain?

To understand the concept of blockchain, you first need to be aware of the importance of currency and its history. Over thousands of years, people from different civilizations have adopted different techniques to create a centralized currency. The main thing that makes a currency usable is the trust which is gained mostly because the government declares it.

Governments first used commodities as an exchange value. Gold is the most famously used exchange value and has been used for hundreds of years. However, over the years, banks began to understand the disadvantages of gold as an exchange value and started to provide paper bills to those who deposited. With time banks began to distribute these notes without any gold deposit, and as it is convenient and comes with trust, all individuals started to use them for exchanging any goods or assets.

Here, the main reason currency works is because of trust. Who provides this trust? A centralized system such as a reserve bank. Every note has a serial number, and this centralized controller has ultimate control over how much money should be printed and any decisions regarding this currency. However, this power gives them absolute control. For example, a couple of years back, India's government announced that the currently valued currency would not be functional anymore, and a new set of currency notes would be distributed. These centralized institutions can sometimes make terrible mistakes, such as printing too many notes, like in Venezuela, which causes inflation to increase and lowers the value of the currency.

Blockchain was fundamentally created to end centralized institutions' monopoly over money management and make currency decentralized. All the transactions that go through a blockchain are publicly available, unlike bank transactions, which are stored on private servers. Right after the 2007-2008 housing crisis in the USA, people realized that banks are untrustworthy and can do anything they want with people's money.

Amid the doubts about these centralized institutions, a whitepaper was published by Satoshi Nakamoto about a cryptocurrency known as Bitcoin. Bitcoin uses the fundamental concept of blockchain and is notably the first popular technology that used it. Since then, the world has changed and can never be the same. Even though blockchain technology was present in 1991, there was no groundbreaking case of its use until the concept of cryptocurrency emerged.

To understand how a blockchain works, you must first understand how centralized institutions such as banks track their records.

How Do Banks Work?

From the beginning, the banks have been used to track the money that is stored in an individual account. Ledgers have transformed from books in which records were entered manually into computers and now into an entirely automatic digital currency system that banks use.

To illustrate this, let's suppose that Tom needs to send a $1000 deposit to his friend Bob. What will he do? He can use either his credit or debit card to send money from his account to Bob's account.

This is what happens:

1. The bank first checks whether the sender has sufficient funds for the transaction to happen.

2. Then, the banking system debits the money from the sender's account and sends it to the receiver's account. Bank servers update the sender's private ledger to reflect the remaining balance present in the account.

3. The receiving account is credited with the $1000 that has been sent. Bank servers update the receiver's private ledger with the updated balance present in the account.

Now that you know how banks work, here are some disadvantages that banks have.

1. Bank servers can be hacked.

2. All your transactions are monitored either by your government or your bank.

3. You can be charged extra fees for not maintaining a minimum account balance.

4. It isn't easy to access the server sometimes when there is heavy traffic.

5. You can be blocked from making certain payments that a bank determines are illegal or prohibited.

As you consider the disadvantages mentioned above, you should now understand that centralized institutions such as banks remove your freedom and allow you to do only what they want you to do. This is indeed problematic.

Now enters the blockchain, which eliminates all these problems. It can make a decentralized system that everyone can use to exchange digital gold and smart contracts or even make decentralized apps that can run in it.

How Does Blockchain Work?

In simple terms, a blockchain is a sequence of blocks that contain any information. These sequences here are called chains.

Blockchains also have something known as a distributed ledger. The most important thing you need to remember about blockchains is that they lock a particular block with cryptographic algorithms whenever data is entered in a blockchain. There is no way to change, alter, or tamper with it.

Why Can't We Change Information in a Block?

The reason blockchains are secure is their use of hashes. A blockchain usually has three important components in it. The first component is data. You can enter data that the blockchain currently supports. Different blockchains allow different data to be entered. For example, with Bitcoin, you can only enter the public addresses of the payer and sender along with the number of coins that are being transferred.

The second component is the hash value that the block has. A hash value is unique, like a fingerprint. Different cryptocurrencies use different hashing algorithms to create a unique hash for each block. They are extremely efficient because whenever data is changed in the block, then the hash value will change automatically.

The third component is the previous hash value. This represents that a chain of blocks is created and when data tampering happens, the hash value will change, and the blocks will no longer be connected.

This technique is the reason blockchains are considered to be extremely secure. Along with hashing techniques, blockchains also use proof of work to effectively reduce the possibility of data in a blockchain being tampered with.

Blockchain Peer-to-Peer Network

Let us suppose that hackers have found a way to calculate the hashes and complete proof of work within less time. Would they then be able to steal your coins?

No, they wouldn't because blockchains add another layer of security by having everything be controlled using a peer-to-peer network instead of being handled by one entity. Here, all the nodes will constantly verify all the blocks present and disagree when there is a block that has been tampered with and will not let it join the blockchain.

What Happens if I Create a New Block?

When you create a new block, it will be sent to every peer present in the network. Now all the peers will verify whether your blockchain is valid or not. If there is any tampered-with data, then the peers in the network will reject the block and will not add it to the blockchain. All these techniques used in blocks make it very difficult to change the data that is present.

Even though blockchain was introduced in 1991, it was ignored until 2008, when Satoshi Nakamoto brought Bitcoin to the public. The invention of Bitcoin made people understand the advantages blockchain provides. Now with smart contracts, decentralized apps, and people trying to create a completely decentralized Internet, blockchain has become the talk of the town.

How Bitcoin Changed Everything

Bitcoin created a decentralized way to transfer money. With Bitcoin, you can no longer be monitored or controlled by a bank. Bitcoin was introduced in 2008 with a whitepaper published anonymously on the Internet by Satoshi Nakamoto.

It didn't gain popularity overnight. People heard about Bitcoin mining at this time, and most of them did it just for fun, but no one ever thought that Bitcoin and its underlying technology would change the world.

Satoshi Nakamoto made the first transaction. He sent 10 BTC to his friend and a developer who helped him to create Bitcoin. However, it did not gain any traction afterward. People just started to mine and used them as a virtual currency in games such as Age of Empires.

When did the first real-world transaction happen?

Until 2010, there were no recorded real-world transactions in the blockchain. Programmers and gamers were just mining Bitcoin on their desktops for fun. The first real word transaction happened when a user in the Bitcoin forum bought two pizzas for 10000 BTC. No one expected this phenomenon to happen so soon.

However, within a few years, Bitcoin became famous worldwide, and many investors and miners started to use it. It became extremely popular on the dark web, where people engaged in illegal trade. Hackers and crackers began to use Bitcoin as a transaction medium because everything is anonymous, and there is no way that third parties can find out who they are.

As of now, in 2021, Bitcoin has reached approximately $50000, and a lot of investors still firmly believe that the good is yet to come, and there will be a lot of attention on it in the future. We arc now just in the initial days of this technology's emergence.

How Does Bitcoin Work?

The only thing that a beginner needs to understand is the concept of decentralized trust in Bitcoin. It is the foundation that made Bitcoin what it is.

A Bitcoin network is a peer-to-peer network where users can make transactions with each other. Every user has a publicly displayed key and a private key that acts as a password. Storing this private key in a suitable place is important if you are serious about working with Bitcoin.

Here is a scenario to help you understand the concept of Bitcoin in an easy way.

Tom is a student at Harvard University. He is studying computer science and has a lot of interest in both cryptocurrency and blockchain. He decides to open a Bitcoin wallet and buys Bitcoin for $1000.

He visits a coffee shop and is surprised to see that the coffee shop now accepts Bitcoin as a payment system. He decides to use his Bitcoin balance to make a payment and drink coffee. He visits the billing system and scans a QR code to pay directly from his Bitcoin wallet to the coffee shop owner's Bitcoin wallet. To make all this happen, Tom had to install a mobile app that allows access to his Bitcoin wallet.

Now, all Tom has to do is enter the amount to be paid, and the system will transfer the Bitcoin to the recipient's account. It looks simple, but it isn't. A lot of stuff goes on in the backend in these few seconds.

Step 1

When Tom scans the QR code, he is automatically entering the public wallet address of the receiver. QR code scanners are made available for automating the process of entering public keys as they are usually hard to type. If you are not comfortable using a QR code scanner, you can manually enter the receiver's public key address.

Step 2

When you enter pay in an app, the process of the transaction will start. It means that all nodes in the network will receive information that a user in the network is trying to send their Bitcoins to another user in the network. Usually, a transaction happens within a few seconds. Whenever a transaction occurs, it will be locked with cryptographic algorithms. Bitcoin uses the SHA-256 hashing algorithm, which is very difficult to crack.

Step 3

Even after a transaction happens, it will not be entered into the public ledger instantly. All the transactions have to be verified using a concept called mining by an individual known as a miner. A miner solves a puzzle or a mathematical problem to place a block of transactions in the blockchain. When they successfully place a block, they will receive the reward in the form of Bitcoin. When your block is placed in the blockchain, there is no way it will get tampered with because of the high-security mechanism blockchains follow.

This is how Bitcoin works from a technical perspective. From a financial perspective, all you need to know is that Bitcoin makes transactions decentralized, and they are also pseudo-anonymous.

What Happened to Satoshi Nakamoto?

Anyone intrigued by the idea of cryptocurrency will be fascinated by the legend of Satoshi Nakamoto. Nobody knows who he is or if he is even a single person. Many have speculated that Satoshi Nakamoto is actually a group of persons that developed Bitcoin and made it available on the Internet.

However, we can understand why Satoshi Nakamoto has chosen to stay anonymous. Bitcoin's popularity has grown tremendously, and if someone knows the owner, he may face problems with both governments and criminals. It is indeed a smart move by Nakamoto to remain anonymous and relax in his pajamas when the world is changing due to his innovation.

Characteristics of Bitcoin

It is Decentralized

The main characteristic of Bitcoin is that no monetary authority controls it. Bitcoin is completely decentralized, and any transaction validated by the blockchain will stay there forever until the blockchain no longer exists. This is quite different from other currencies that are controlled by central banks. There is no control over Bitcoin, and all the cryptocurrency that is distributed will be either sold or bought only by the people involved. No institution can make your Bitcoins lose value like how they do to normal currency. Bitcoin is a community-driven digital currency.

There is a Limited Supply

The amount of Bitcoin that can circulate is fixed, unlike that of traditional currency that can be printed whenever a centralized institution needs to. Inflation is an important concept that investors should understand before judging the limited circulation of Bitcoin.

The number of Bitcoins that can be made is capped at 21 million. However, Bitcoin researchers have found that we can circulate Bitcoin by dividing it, and the division can go as far as eight decimal places. In fact, people do buy fractional Bitcoins, which makes the currency more accessible to less wealthy investors.

It can be quite hard for a beginner to understand, but Bitcoin can never fall victim to inflation thanks to this mechanism. People will continue mining Bitcoins for the time being, but the supply will probably run out within the next 20 years.

Bitcoin Cannot Be Forged or Reversed

All the transactions that are made in the blockchain use strict cryptographic algorithms to secure it. As soon as you make a transaction, it will be locked and forever inserted into the blockchain. You can also not make the same multiple transactions because you need to wait a certain amount of time to validate the transaction.

Whenever you make a transaction in a Bitcoin blockchain, the sender can never reverse it. If you want the value back, then you need to ask the receiver to make another transaction to your Bitcoin wallet. All these characteristics can help users in the blockchain make trustful and worthy exchanges.

Transactions are Completely Anonymous

There is no way to discern who the account holder of a Bitcoin wallet is by using its address unless they decide to reveal who they are. This anonymity gives you various advantages. Bitcoin became popular because people on the darknet started to use it for mostly illegal exchanges.

Bitcoin also allows you to not pay taxes if you don't want to. According to the IRS, only 800 Bitcoin investors paid income tax on their investments in 2020. The ethical concerns that arise from Bitcoin's anonymity are a hugely controversial topic. However, Bitcoin enthusiasts should focus on the advantages instead of the disadvantages it may come with.

Transactions Can Be Sent Anywhere in the World

Bitcoin has nodes in all countries in the world. Mining is popular everywhere, and thus your location doesn't matter. All Bitcoin transactions take a few seconds to happen and take 10 minutes at the most to get validated and inserted in the blockchain. You can send it to any person in the world, and you will be charged the same transaction fee no matter the destination. With Bitcoin, you no longer have the problem of exchange rates that apply when you make a foreign transaction with your bank.

Bitcoin has made blockchain technology popular and since then has been used by different companies to create different cryptocurrencies. All these cryptocurrencies work well because they support a public ledger system that validates the transactions by mining. Understanding Bitcoin mining can help you understand the importance of miners in the crypto world.

Chapter 2: Understanding Technicalities of Bitcoin

Bitcoin and blockchain are both boons for investors and computer programmers. While programmers can develop a robust and breathtaking decentralized application using these technologies, investors can bet on these technologies to change the world. Both investors and programmers balance the landscape of cryptocurrency. This chapter will explain various important concepts that a Bitcoin investor needs to be aware of. Follow along!

What Is Bitcoin Mining?

There is no correlation between how actual mining and digital mining work. Bitcoin mining is a complex process and uses a concept known as proof of work to make new Bitcoins come into circulation. Mining right now can be done only by computers that can handle a lot of computer power and energy.

Satoshi Nakamoto designed the Bitcoin blockchain system to make it more and more difficult to mine a block as time goes on. Nakamoto's idea was to stop the production of Bitcoins early and prevent its inflation.

In 2021, only a few miners get all the rewards because only they have equipment that can handle the enormous load that comes with verifying complex mathematical problems or puzzles.

Even if Bitcoin mining is unrewarding right now, many still believe that even these pennies they get as a reward after mining can increase their value over time. The primary purpose of Bitcoin mining is to validate the transactions that occur in the blockchain ecosystem. This validation is essential because Bitcoin is a decentralized system, and this validation is what makes it secure and keeps it from being tampered with. In real-world terms, Bitcoin miners can be called auditors for the blockchain ecosystem.

Bitcoin mining was introduced to tackle the double-spending problem. With centralized digital currency systems, there is a ledger, and miners verify everything. There is no chance of counterfeiting or sending the same money over and over. However, with Bitcoins, people are sending the same Bitcoin to different users in the network. Miners come in the middle to check these transactions and make sure that the hashes are not repeated. Miners usually need to complete 1MB of transactions to complete a block in the blockchain.

Is Bitcoin Mining Practical?

To be frank, it's subjective. Many miners believe that the mining system is inherently flawed because it favors people with high equipment to mine faster instead of individuals. In Bitcoin mining, solving mathematical problems is just equal to taking guesses of the hashes. Usually, the computer needs to make trillions of guesses to mine a block. Both effort and luck come in place when mining the blocks.

To solve this problem, individuals have started using pools to compete with other prominent players in the mining industry. What these pools essentially do is combine all their power and use it to mine a block. In this way, the probability of reaching the correct hash increases. When pools get a reward, miners share the reward among all of their members based on the energy consumption by a specific individual.

How Many Bitcoins Can Be Produced?

Bitcoin miners are an essential part of the blockchain ecosystem. If all the miners stop doing what they do, the system will collapse, and there will be no way to verify the transactions in the blockchain.

Unlike that of centralized currency, the circulation of Bitcoin is not unlimited. It is capped at just 21 million. As of this writing, 18.5 million Bitcoins have already been mined, and it has become difficult to mine a single block. However, remember that due to Bitcoin standards, the complete mining of 21 million blocks will likely not happen until 2140.

How Much of a Reward Can a Miner Earn?

Satoshi Nakamoto used a concept known as Bitcoin halving to increase the value of Bitcoin over time. In 2009, when Bitcoin mining was first introduced, you needed to wait 10 minutes to mine 50 blocks. But the system is designed in such a way that Bitcoin halving will occur approximately every four years. In 2012, the number was reduced to 25 blocks for 10 minutes of mining. In 2016, it declined to 12.5 blocks.

Right now, in 2021, Bitcoin miners can only start circulating 6.25 BTC in 10 minutes. With the reduction in the circulation of new Bitcoins, the already existing Bitcoins in circulation will increase in value. There is no wonder that many researchers and financial analysts are expecting Bitcoin to reach 1 million dollars by 2030.

Bitcoin Mining and Controversies

A lot of people believe that Bitcoin mining involves a lot of consumption of power and energy. People are mining worldwide with their expensive ASIC (application-specific integrated circuit) computers to validate transactions in an isolated digital currency platform.

While there is debate about how miners use power and energy, many miners are using renewable resources to mine and circulate new Bitcoin blocks. However, with time, Bitcoin mining will have problems related to power consumption, and to counter this problem, new concepts such as proof of stake are being developed in various other cryptocurrencies.

Bitcoin Mining and Scams

With the tremendous opportunities Bitcoin mining provides, a lot of individuals are exploiting the system. For example, you might have seen advertisements of different cloud miners who promise that you can get valid returns by renting their servers and mining using a web client. These offers are scams and are worthless.

Proof of Work Vs. Proof of Stake

Proof of work makes miners solve mathematical problems to make everyone in the network verify that the transaction is valid. With proof of stake, individuals earn the right to mine a particular block by staking the money.

The proof of stake mechanism asks individuals who are interested in mining the coins for some of the coins in their wallets and takes that stake of coins to give the prospective miner the ability to mine. Cryptocurrencies such as Cardano and Polkadot are introducing this concept into their blockchain platforms. With a debate growing around the effects of Bitcoin mining, green cryptocurrencies will have a massive demand in the future.

How to Start Using Bitcoin

To enter the beautiful world of Bitcoin, all you need to do is install a client. There are clients for every platform, such as web, desktop, and mobile. Choosing a client is also a difficult and overwhelming choice nowadays because there are hundreds of apps and software. We suggest you check public user reviews to judge which one is better for you.

Different type of clients available:

Full Client

This is the type of client that many Bitcoin enthusiasts will recommend to you. When you download a full client and install it, all the transactions that ever happened in the blockchain will be downloaded to your computer. This usually takes a lot of time. Right now, you need almost 350GB of storage to download all the completed transactions in the blockchain.

Light Client

When you use a light client, you will have access to all the transactions that have occurred, but for the most part, you will need to rely on private servers of data for these clients.

Web Client

This is just like using a PayPal account. All you need to do is enter your public and private addresses to open your Bitcoin wallet and do whatever transaction you need to do.

Mobile Client

Some mobile clients can do everything a full, lightweight, or web wallet can do. However, they are not portable and may cause issues as most of these are open-source projects and may have bugs and vulnerabilities.

What Client Should I Choose?

It is entirely dependent on your purpose. If you are a Bitcoin miner, then it is evident that you need to depend on a full client as you will be verifying and validating all the new transactions in the blockchain. A lightweight client is an obvious choice for anyone who is just starting.

Web clients are controversial because even though they provide immediate access, they are more prone to phishing and Trojan attacks. It is your responsibility to carefully manage your account not to fall prey to these attacks.

Sending and Receiving Bitcoins

We will use Multibit, a lightweight client, to explain how to send and receive Bitcoins. We will explain step-by-step to help beginners understand the exact procedure.

Download the Client

First, visit the official website of Multibit to download the program. It is available for all operating systems including Windows, Linux, and Mac. Download and install it with administrative privileges.

Note: You need to use a password for your wallet. This is mandatory. Make sure that you select a password that is tough to crack. Using common words or very weak passwords that can easily be hacked using a brute force attack is a big **NO**.

Open the Client

After installation, when you open the client, you will be welcomed with a popup. It will ask you to agree to its privacy policies. Make sure you read them to understand how different clients use your data. Some clients are said to have some dubious policies, so it is recommended to cross-check to avoid future problems.

When you first open your client, it will automatically generate a Bitcoin address and wallet for you. You can send the given Bitcoin address to anyone to receive money in Bitcoins. Multibit also provides a QR code scanner to make transactions seamless.

Send and Receive Bitcoins

Now, when you install, the client will generate a public address and private key. However, until you make a valid transaction, your address will not be entered into the public ledger. Until you make a transaction, your wallet address is a random address out of countless possible addresses.

To send and receive Bitcoin addresses, each party needs to have a Bitcoin address. The address is also necessary to use trading platforms to understand the current price of Bitcoin and how many Bitcoins you need to send to the receiver.

For example, at the time of writing, $100 equals 0.0022 Bitcoin. These rates will be changing constantly as cryptocurrencies are highly volatile. After knowing the exact number of Bitcoins you need to send, you can enter the address and number of Bitcoins and seamlessly send them. It will, however, take 10 minutes for miners to validate your transaction. When it does, your address will forever be placed in the blockchain, and all the peers in the network will know your identity whenever a subsequent transaction takes place, and anyone in the network can check your transactions. You will not have privacy, but you can be anonymous, and you can hide your real identity.

How to Get Your First Bitcoins

In the early days, people used to get Bitcoins by mining them. But as Bitcoin started to gain fame, many cryptocurrency exchanges such as Coinbase started to provide Bitcoins to their user base when they deposit regular currency.

They act much in the same way as brokers for stock investors and charge a small transaction fee when you try to liquidate your Bitcoins into your regular currency. Right now, there are more than 20 trusted cryptocurrency exchanges in the US. Coinbase and Binance are the most popular among them.

You can also get Bitcoin from non-crypto specific exchanges that also allow stock trading. Webull and Robinhood are popular choices, and they offer other cryptocurrencies as well.

We suggest you do thorough research before proceeding further. Also, remember that to open accounts on these platforms, you need to provide a valid social security number and identifying documents.

When Not to Buy Cryptocurrency

It is also worth mentioning some instances when you should not risk investing in cryptocurrencies.

1. When you are not confident about your investment choice

2. When there is extreme volatility in the market

3. When you have not done thorough research about a particular cryptocurrency

All these technicalities have helped Blockchain technology and Bitcoin to become popular among technological enthusiasts. The success of Bitcoin made the Blockchain revolution a reality and is now being hailed as one of the revolutions that has a huge potential to change the world. An overview of the Blockchain revolution can help crypto enthusiasts understand the core philosophical goals of cryptocurrencies.

Chapter   3:   Blockchain Revolution

Blockchain has changed the world in a lot of different ways. The concept of decentralization has spread because of the invention of Bitcoin in 2008 by Satoshi Nakomoto. The impact of blockchain, Bitcoin, and other cryptocurrencies is highly remarkable from both a technological and financial perspective. The blockchain revolution is still ongoing, and in the coming years, we can experience its overall impact on society. This chapter will provide valuable information about some insights into the blockchain revolution with concrete examples. Follow along!

What Is Digital Currency?

The concept of digital currency emerged during the recession of 2007-2008. People lost their trust in banks and were looking for other alternatives to invest their money. Banks have come a long way from depositing gold to making unwise decisions that can cause an economic collapse. The 2008 recession is especially important for a cryptocurrency enthusiast because it spurred investors and non-investors alike to think of alternatives to the economic system that had failed so many people.

In 2008, when Bitcoin was invented to fight the centralization of banks, people were overwhelmed. Until then, there was little discussion about digital currency or blockchain, even on the Internet. Many programmers and investors slowly observed the rising phenomenon and started to understand the advantages cryptocurrency provides.

A cryptocurrency is a form of digital currency that can only exist on the Internet. Services like bank-issued virtual currency fall under this category. The fundamental difference between these services and cryptocurrency is that cryptocurrency systems have a public ledger, and it is tough for anyone to alter the blockchain.

We will first explain the impact of centralized digital currency and its effect on the economy with clear examples. We will also mention instances where blockchain can revolutionize the world for the better. Follow along!

Digital Currency Revolution

For thousands of years, banks have controlled money and its circulation. Every country has a reserve bank, and it decides, depending on various factors, how much currency should be printed. Excessive printing of notes can lead to higher inflation and increase the cost of products. This happened quite recently in Zimbabwe and Venezuela.

Digital currency emerged in the 2000s but became famous only after the invention of Bitcoin. Banks started to provide digital online transfers 24/7 to any domestic account. Each country adapted its digital currency algorithm for its users. For example, Alibaba is a digital payment system that changed the Chinese economy. Now, approximately a billion users are using Alibaba all around their world for day-to-day transactions.

While digital currency has its advantages, there are also many disadvantages from a crypto enthusiast's perspective. The government can monitor all your transactions, and sometimes they can even decide to block you from purchasing a specific product or service due to this centralization of currency.

Digital currency is innovative, easy to use, and is logically a good idea for connecting people. However, it still has its disadvantages, and a cryptocurrency can solve all these because no one has absolute control over it.

Blockchain Revolution

People who believe in the blockchain revolution are heavily optimistic that it will change the world into a better place. The main feature they believe to be an advantage for blockchain is its decentralization capability. They assert that blockchain technology can eliminate corruption and help people all around the world make everything safe because all the data in a blockchain is available publicly for anyone to investigate.

For blockchains, accountability is not only a feature, but it is also their goal. All crypto enthusiasts believe that blockchain technology can eliminate the middlemen that are currently the obstacles preventing an economic boom. It could destroy all centralized institutions that lead to corruption and inflation in a country. The power of governments, multinational companies, would decrease over time, and the power of individuals would increase.

These claims may sound either utopian or dystopian, depending on an individual's perspective. We will cover what cryptocurrency has to offer and how that could make the world a better place.

How Can Blockchain Technology Revolutionize the Health and Food Industries?

Health and food are vital industries that everyone in the world depends upon. They are billion-dollar industries and are non-cyclic as there will always be demand for them. blockchain technologies can make all health systems completely transparent since the government cannot alter the data in any way.

Blockchain technology can also help doctors and other health personnel effectively manage health reports and data that patients provide. We can use this abundant data to develop blockchain platforms that can predict and estimate diseases that can occur for an individual depending on their health habits or food purchases.

To help you understand more about this idea, we will provide a simple example.

Let us suppose that you bought organic vegetables from Walmart every day for almost a year. After a year, let us assume that you became hospitalized with a severe stomachache. After a complete examination, doctors informed you that you have severe problems in your kidney, and surgery is necessary to eliminate further complications.

After a successful surgery, you decided to change your food habits and choose not to use organic vegetables because you firmly believed that they were the reason for your health complications that arose. You decided to research where they are being imported from.

You reached out to Walmart and interviewed officials to learn the details about the company that imported the vegetables. There will be a middleman in any business, and to reach the farm where the vegetables are grown, you figure that you need to spend at least seven days chasing the supply chain. There is no way to verify whether intermediaries are telling you the truth.

Now, do you know how much time it would take to verify what farm the vegetables came from if you use blockchain technology? Just a second or two.

It would be easy to track because the data in the blockchain is linked whenever new data is added and cannot be altered in any way. We can precisely estimate the number of units that were exported and the date farmers exported them. This will not only reduce corruption but would also help you to verify whether you are using up-to-date products effectively. Blockchain improves transparency in a way that no other technology of this generation can provide.

How Can Blockchain Revolutionize the Internet?

The Internet is a wild place. There are many ways you can utilize, learn about, and experiment with the enormous powers of the Internet. However, just a few superpowers control the Internet. A small number of tech companies such as Google and Facebook govern most of the services you use from social media to e-mail to e-commerce.

Everyone now knows the importance of privacy, but there is still a lot of hard work and time needed to make everything right with the Internet.

Blockchain is just the right technology to decentralize the Internet effectively. The power of tech companies will decrease, and the power of individuals will increase with the help of blockchain technology. Ethereum, a popular blockchain platform, allows programmers to create decentralized apps that can reduce the big players' control over individuals. There is still a long way to go, but with the ongoing blockchain revolution, it doesn't take much time to understand its capabilities.

What can be achieved?

You can easily rent or buy fine storage from individuals for low prices instead of depending on multinational companies such as Dropbox. Artists, photographers, and authors can sell their products without facing a cut in their royalties. Programmers can sell their licensed code or products and apps individually with less outside control over them. whether

Blockchain's goal for the Internet is simple. Blockchain can give us a clean Internet that increases individual freedom and that eliminates the control of big players.

How Can Blockchain Revolutionize the Automobile Industry?

The automobile industry is essential for the economy. For over 100 years, despite war and recession, the automobile industry has thrived. Several people have proposed the idea of linking blockchain to autonomous automobiles.

The basic idea is that vehicles would be able to communicate and decide whether the communication is reliable based on different blockchain apps. The idea is still being developed and may still take a little time to become a practical alternative. Now, electric cars are booming, and many are advocating autopilot driving. Using autonomous blockchain practices can change the world for the better by reducing accidents and eliminating situations such as robbery and driving while drunk. We suggest you read some of the peer-reviewed journals published on this concept to understand more about it.

How Can Blockchain Increase Renewable Energy?

This is controversial, and we are sure that there are many varied and nuanced opinions on this topic. There are two types of energy: renewable and non-renewable. Many people depend heavily on non-renewable sources to produce electricity because it is efficient and can bring power to a lot of people. Electricity produced with coal is a perfect example of this.

Renewable sources of energy, on the other hand, require an initial investment to integrate them with existing systems and are not entirely reliable because there may be interruptions to their availability. Solar energy is a perfect example of this.

Now, cryptocurrencies require specific individuals known as miners to validate the transactions. Validating transactions requires miners to solve complex mathematical problems, which takes a lot of energy and electricity. As of this writing, it is said that more than 75% of Bitcoin miners are using renewable sources of energy to validate transactions.

While there is no official way to confirm this, energy experts are still optimistic that the world sees demand for renewable energy sources due to the blockchain revolution.

How Can Blockchain Revolutionize Politics and Prevent Wars?

Politics is a sensitive topic and differs from country to country depending on economic and constitutional laws. Using blockchain, we can find a transparent way to track what governments are doing worldwide. We can also effectively track digital currency so it is not used to sponsor wars.

Governments can also use blockchain technology for voting to ensure that each citizen gets only one chance to vote. Rigging and malpractices in an election system, especially in underdeveloped or developing countries, can be eliminated using blockchain technology.

How Can Blockchain Revolutionize the Copyright System?

Copyright is important to intellectual property owners such as writers and artists. On the Internet, it is easy to steal intellectual property from each other with just a few clicks. When someone steals another's work, the creator needs first to send an e-mail or letter to the imposter and request that they discontinue their use of the stolen work. The creator can sue if they don't respond with a valid reason.

This all takes a lot of time, and the copyright owner has to spend a lot on legal fees. With blockchain technology, we can eliminate intermediaries in this process. All you need to do is create an intellectual piece of work and immediately create a timestamp and insert all the data or details of the work into the blockchain. Based on the data that is present, the blockchain generates a unique hash code.

With your unique hash code, you can now easily sue or press charges on anyone who steals or copies your work without permission. This can also be used in the music industry to establish ownership rights to songs.

How Can Blockchain Revolutionize Healthcare?

Right now, health is everyone's priority. All the health records that are usually collected in hospitals stay isolated, and they are not publicly available for research purposes. A lot of health services can be improved by effectively integrating with different decentralized blockchain platforms.

Using blockchain, users in the network can create a DNA wallet where everything related to your health data would be stored. This data cannot be altered or tampered with in any way. So there would be a lot of transparent data that researchers can utilize. In the real world, a lot of reports are faked or manipulated for many reasons. Having reliable health data can be a life-saving thing, especially during pandemics such as COVID-19.

Incorporating blockchain with pharmaceutical products can also help you reduce the impact of counterfeiting drugs. All you would need to do is verify it using a blockchain platform and learn where it was manufactured. This can reduce both the black market and ineffective drugs usually put on the market to make some quick gains.

How Can Blockchain Revolutionize IoT?

The Internet of Things is still in its early stages, but it has massive potential in the future. With the Internet of Things, you can interact with various products in your home or at work through your Internet connection. The Internet of Things reduces stress and introduces a whole new digital world that makes your life easier.

We can now introduce blockchain technology to each of these platforms to make a chain of networks that can interact. IoT blockchain companies such as Helium are finding ways to create a real-world decentralized network that can interact with routers and other electronic peripherals that are around.

How Can Blockchain Revolutionize Agriculture?

Agriculture can be greatly impacted by blockchain technology. Agriculture is filled with intermediaries who make demands of the farmers, depending on the supply. When there is a lot of supply, farmers are usually forced to provide their products for a significantly lower price.

The problem for farmers is highly relevant in underdeveloped countries. Blockchain technology can help eliminate this middleman and help farmers interact directly with small, local shops or large stores like Walmart. Blockchain technology would also benefit the consumer because all the data would be entered into the blockchain, and anyone would be able to verify the farm where their food is produced.

Developers can also create various decentralized applications to link agriculture and finance.

How Can Blockchain Revolutionize Charities?

Right now, on the Internet, charities are being controlled by websites such as GoFundMe. They are good initiatives, but they do charge a fee for every campaign. With blockchain, we can create technologies that can reduce these charges and easily send money to people in need.

Non-profit organizations can also stop depending on banks and other financial institutions and can make their transactions using blockchain technology.

Can Cryptocurrency Be a Logical Replacement for USD?

There are a lot of differences between traditional currency and digital currencies such as Bitcoin. Many crypto investors firmly believe that Bitcoin and other cryptocurrencies can effectively replace the US dollar (USD). Cryptocurrencies are more transparent, easy to use, and are safer. Crypto is decentralized, and no one can control your money.

But let us look at this logically. Can we live without fiat currency and depend entirely on digital currency? It's unlikely. Believing that cryptocurrencies can eliminate traditional money is over-optimism. The main reason currency works is trust, and cryptos have a lot of work to do to create the trust that the public has for their local fiat currencies.

At this moment, the cryptocurrency market is considered volatile and risky. People are not entirely aware of the power of decentralization, and it may take a lot of time to make every person on the planet understand it.

Also, there is an ethical problem with cryptocurrency. If the future that crypto enthusiasts dream of indeed comes true, then many who work in centralized institutions such as banks will lose their jobs. How can crypto coins find a solution for this? We don't know yet. The future of cryptocurrency is intriguing and exciting to follow, but purely from a philosophical perspective, trying to destroy centralization is not its goal. Making decentralized technology and currency available to people who need it is the primary goal of cryptocurrency.

Governments' Plans for Cryptocurrency

Governments around the world are calmly observing the rise of cryptocurrency. Some countries like China are, however, vocal about their disapproval of cryptocurrencies in general. Presently, all governments are considering different ways to reduce the usage of cryptocurrency by investors.

However, no government can make cryptocurrency illegal because many retail investors and businesses are now entirely dependent on it. Doing so would cause a huge controversy and could lead to immense criticism.

Cryptocurrency is a great technology, but it targets all centralized institutions. Whether or not everyone agrees, Satoshi Nakamoto created a system that can cripple banks and intermediaries who are the reason for corruption and many other problems that the world faces today. Cryptocurrency is definitely on government hit lists, but the fall of crypto will not happen anytime soon.

The blockchain revolution can lead to financial independence for thousands of investors all around the world. Being a crypto investor requires a lot of skills and strategies that an individual needs to be aware of. For an investor, choosing the right cryptocurrencies after a thorough fundamental analysis is an important undertaking.

Chapter 4: Understanding Crypto Investment

We now have good knowledge about the technical side of blockchain. For financial investment choices, we need to know about the different opportunities that cryptocurrency platforms can provide. This chapter will talk about various trading strategies and detailed fundamental analysis tactics that investors can use. Please remember that these strategies can never guarantee you profits. Always make investment choices only after thorough research.

Understanding Cryptocurrency Trading Strategies

Cryptocurrency trading is volatile and unpredictable. To stay in the game, you need to plan wisely and be aware of different strategies that a crypto investor can use to make profits. A lot of the content mentioned below coincides with stock market investing. To be a successful cryptocurrency trader, we suggest you try different strategies and stick to the one you are most comfortable with. Ensure that you have a sufficient understanding of technical and fundamental analysis as all these trading strategies require you to know these types of analysis for good gains.

Why Is a Trading Strategy Necessary?

With a clear strategy, profits can't be guaranteed, but you can effectively minimize your losses. The main reason every investor uses a plan is to not fall prey to sudden movements, which could lead to a roller coaster of emotions. In these moments, having a clear plan can help you maintain peace of mind and make impressive decisions that can help you maintain your financial stability.

A plan usually consists of the following information :

1. When to start and end a trade

2. What tools can be used to help you trade

3. Which chart patterns you need to focus primarily on for this trade

4. Whether you should use stop losses

5. How to record the performance of your portfolio

A plan can also consist of psychological points that help you consider what will not work for you. Using these as reminders can help you to focus more on your target.

In the next section, we will talk about some of the famous cryptocurrency investing strategies that traders use worldwide. Always choose what you wish to do based on personal preferences.

Cryptocurrency Trading and Investing Strategies

Day Trading

Day trading is derived from stock markets where investors sell all the assets they have bought within that same day, not worrying about losses. Usually, this is called intraday trading in stock market terms. The SEC also allows traders in the stock market to participate in day trading. However, investors can only day trade on the stock market if they have a portfolio worth over $25,0000 because the practice is considered too risky for less wealthy investors to engage in. However, with cryptocurrencies' lack of a centralized authority, you can start day trading with much less capital. This can be a boon for investors who would rather focus on short-term gains, but potential traders should make sure to weigh the risks of each trade.

Another way day trading in cryptocurrency is different from day trading in stocks is that cryptocurrencies trade 24 hours a day, seven days a week, with no break. Day traders involved in cryptocurrency tend to buy and sell the coins within 24 hours or less, while stock traders have less than eight hours a day to conduct day trades and can't day trade during the weekend.

A day trader is highly dependent on charts and advanced technical analysis methods to estimate price fluctuations.

Should I be involved in day trading?

While it is easy to start with day trading, it is still not for beginners as it involves many risks. Advanced traders can, however, utilize their technical analysis skills to predict cryptocurrency trends.

Swing Trading

Swing trading is the most recommended cryptocurrency strategy for beginners. The concept of swing trading emerged after the dot-com bust and since then has been popular in stock investing. Cryptocurrency traders also started to use swing trading techniques to predict price changes from a day to no more than two months.

As a swing trader, you need to understand both fundamental and technical analysis techniques and implement them while estimating the swings. Swing trading works very well for cryptocurrency traders as there is a lot of volatility. You make decisions only when there is a real price change instead of panic pumping or dumping coins because of short-term price changes.

Should I be involved in swing trading?

If you are a beginner and are very confident about your fundamental and technical skills, then this is a good strategy for you to gain initial profits.

Position Trading

Not all traders depend on short-term trading strategies to raise income. A lot of crypto investors use position trading to hold these coins for at least a few months. Trend trading (also known as position trading) is popular because it guarantees investors with excellent fundamental analysis skills have huge returns.

Being patient and carefully observing any black swan or megatrends during this time is an essential skill for position traders.

Should I be involved in position trading?

As a position trader, you need to be aware of long-term investment choices. Position trading is a perfect choice to get potential high returns over a long time.

Buy-and-Hold Investing

There is a slight difference between position traders and buy-and-hold investors. The time difference dramatically increases for the latter. They don't consider any market factors while starting to invest in a cryptocurrency. They also do not bother themselves with any technical indicators such as charts or price swings because they don't matter in the long term.

All their focus stands upon the future of the particular cryptocurrency they are investing in. They do complete research and compile it to judge whether it is a viable investment.

Index Investing

This is a new investment method in which investors start to invest in a set of cryptocurrencies by forming a separate index. It is not quite popular, but investors predict that it will be a big thing in the future because cryptocurrencies are developing relationships among themselves and the blockchains are slowly becoming less isolated. It may take time, but index investing is a must-know for every crypto enthusiast.

Scalping

Scalpers are traders who heavily depend on the inefficiencies of a cryptocurrency. Scalpers usually have a considerable volume of assets and carefully observe market conditions using different indicators such as technical analysis, market conditions, and influencers to decide when to buy or sell.

Scalping strategies are pretty tricky to understand because every investor makes their decisions in a few seconds. For beginners, we don't recommend scalping because it is highly risky.

Of course, to fully form a trading strategy, you need relevant skills to support the strategy, and one of the most important skills is the ability to analyze the markets.

Fundamental Analysis for Cryptocurrency Investors

Every investor, regardless of the financial instrument they have chosen, should have some knowledge of fundamental analysis to estimate whether an asset is a good buy at a particular price point. In a highly volatile market, many factors affect price changes, and understanding these factors can help a fundamental analyst correctly determine whether an asset is either undervalued or overvalued.

Both technical and fundamental analysis should be used to make a valuable investing choice. Technical analysis can be used to predict future price movements. On the other hand, fundamental analysis helps you analyze whether the price of the cryptocurrency right now is the asset's actual value.

Technical analysis in cryptocurrency is similar to the way traders use it to predict price movements in stocks, derivatives, or commodities. All trading platforms and technical analysis software are now providing cryptocurrency charts and statistics to attract more investors.

On the other hand, fundamental analysis is considered more difficult with cryptocurrencies than with other financial instruments because a lot of centralized factors such as inflation, depletion rates, and economic reforms don't impact the price of the cryptocurrency. However, a single tweet from an influential figure like Elon Musk can cause a drastic change in a cryptocurrency's market performance. To completely understand the fundamental analysis of cryptocurrencies, you need to be aware of most of the mentioned factors below.

Factors That an Investor Needs to Be Aware of

1. **On-Chain Metrics**

   Every blockchain is a public ledger. All the data in the blockchain is publicly available for everyone to either watch or analyze using complex software to understand how a cryptocurrency is trading.

   It is difficult for an average investor to extract all the on-chain metrics at once, so we recommend you use different APIs to extract this information for your fundamental analysis.

   a. **Transaction Count and Value**

   Both transaction count and value can be considered excellent factors to judge current cryptocurrency values. Transaction count refers to the number of transactions that happen overall for a network in 24 hours. Whereas the transaction value refers to the total amount that has been exchanged in 24 hours.

Note: Remember, investors cannot solely use transaction count or value for fundamental analysis because many big players send money to their different wallets to manipulate the current value of their cryptocurrency. This especially happens with newly created altcoins.

b. Active Addresses

A lot of value in cryptocurrency exists because of long-term investors. However, they usually become inactive after a time and cannot help a fundamental analyst precisely estimate the asset's value. This is why you need to find the active addresses based on both senders and receiver accounts over some time.

c. Fees Paid

Mining is an essential procedure for a cryptocurrency to validate the transactions that have occurred. To validate these transactions, an individual must pay a fee, which goes to the cryptocurrency miner as a reward. This procedure is known as proof of work, and it has made cryptocurrencies what they are now.

As a fundamental analyst, you need to check whether the transaction value has increased or not as the reward for a miner shrinks considerably over time due to blockchain halving. If the transaction value doesn't change, then the miner is working for a loss and will leave soon, thus making the blockchain less secure.

d. Hash Rate

Hashing is the combination of complex algorithms that cryptocurrencies use to secure the information in the blockchain. The increase in hash rate is directly proportional to the rise in the security of the blockchain. An increase in hash rate also can be understood as a popularity index for the cryptocurrency as thousands of miners are busy validating the transactions.

You can use trading software and many websites on the Internet to analyze other less popular on-chain metrics that can help you evaluate cryptocurrency. These indicators can only help you estimate whether a particular blockchain is a valuable asset or not. To move further and analyze cryptocurrency projects that you want to invest in, follow the below-mentioned project metrics.

2. Project Metrics

With the help of the development of the Ethereum blockchain, smart contracts have emerged. With these smart contracts, you can start projects and create an ICO (initial coin offerings) to raise capital for an ambitious cryptocurrency project.

A lot of cryptocurrency investors suggest you participate in ICOs to get higher returns over time. As a fundamental analyst, you need to analyze the following factors to estimate whether a project is a valuable investment or a probable scam.

a. The Whitepaper

A whitepaper is a technical document that shares general information about the project. It provides a lot of information about the team that is developing the project and mentions the goal they are trying to achieve.

Here are some things you need to remember:

Check whether the project is confidential. If it is open-source, you will have an advantage as the project development phase will be transparent.

Understand the project's main goal and the target demographics.

Make sure that you get information about developers' thoughts about future updates. This is especially important for a business to maintain sustained growth.

b. The Team and Their Capabilities

Research, the team that is mentioned in the whitepaper. Look at their GitHub profiles to determine whether they have the experience to complete this project. Also, find some open websites where people make lists of scammers who have created fraudulent ICOs for quick gains.

Always use common sense before judging whether a project can work out. A lot of ICOs start with initial funding but can't survive because the team behind it doesn't have enough technical knowledge or skills to move the project forward.

c. Competitors and Their Work

Understand the area that you are targeting and find both private and public information about their competitors. Understanding competition can help you to determine a proposed project's likelihood of success. For a fundamental analyst, this is an important part of ascertaining the value of the project.

d. Initial Distribution

As an investor, you need to focus on the tokens that these projects provide for their investors. It is also essential to do quick research on the number of people who may have invested. If there are only a few investors with high capital, it is a risky investment.

Understand that even by analyzing all these project metrics, there is a chance that you will invest in a business that is either a scam or created by not-so-focused developers. We will be discussing ICOs in the later chapters of this book to help you judge whether to invest in a new project.

3. Financial Metrics

These are critical metrics a fundamental analyst must analyze before determining the correct value of a cryptocurrency.

a. Market Capitalization

Market capitalization is an essential metric for any financial security. For cryptocurrencies, however, the market capitalization is not easy to estimate as many coins are either burned or inactive because of lost keys.

Market capitalization can be defined as the multiplication of circulating supply with the current price of the cryptocurrency. As said before, this will only provide an estimation for a fundamental analyst. However, market capitalization is especially important to prove that a coin is a success.

b. Liquidity and Volume

Liquidity determines the ability to either sell or buy the asset whenever you like. For example, if you buy some of the unpopular coins, then you may face liquidity problems because most of the time, there may not be a buyer who will take them at the price you set. To make a sale at any cost, you may need to decrease your price or wait until the cryptocurrency's liquidity increases.

Volume is directly proportional to liquidity. When there is a huge day trading volume, then it is highly possible that you can either buy or sell the asset for your asking price. All popular currencies such as Bitcoin, Ethereum, Litecoin, and XRP have high volume and liquidity.

Combining All These Metrics

As a fundamental analyst, you need to combine all three of these factors and judge whether the current price matches the cryptocurrency's actual value. If you don't find the price reasonable, wait until the price dips over time and then join the blockchain. It is always better to combine technical analysis techniques with fundamental analysis to have more fruitful results in cryptocurrency investment.

Understanding Crypto Exchanges

As an investor, you might already know that both investing and trading of cryptocurrencies happen online most of the time. Brick-and-mortar cryptocurrency exchanges exist but don't have much of a demand. People use online cryptocurrency exchanges because they work better and are more convenient.

What are crypto exchanges?

The fundamental principle of crypto exchanges is that they can help people exchange their fiat currency into cryptocurrencies and vice versa. Many exchanges also allow investors to convert their cryptocurrency to other cryptos without fiat currency.

For example, with a crypto exchange, you can liquidate your Bitcoins to exchange them for Ethereum coins.

But remember that the exchange will charge you a transaction fee.

What are the different types of crypto exchanges?

Centralized Crypto Exchanges (CCE)

Centralized crypto exchanges just act like regular stock exchanges. When you trade or invest with a centralized crypto exchange, it acts as a mediator between you and the other party who is willing to buy or sell according to your wishes. For this procedure, these exchanges charge a commission.

Right now, with the exponential growth of the cryptocurrency market, there has been an increase in crypto exchanges, and choosing which ones to use can be a daunting task.

What to be aware of while selecting a centralized crypto exchange?

- *Security*

Security is essential for any exchange that handles your money and cryptocurrencies. Make sure that the exchanges provide 2FA(two-factor authentication) along with cold storage for all your data.

- *Liquidity*

How much liquidity an exchange offers becomes important, especially during a highly volatile market day when there is a lot of panic selling.

- *Commission Fees*

Having a reasonable commission fee is important, especially if you are a day trader. For a long-term investor, commission fees can be less important.

- *Excellent UI*

In today's technological world, a clean and beautiful interface has become mandatory for any business.

- *Payment Options*

A good crypto exchange should provide various options to both deposit and withdraw money.

- *Customer Support*

Computers are not always perfect, and you may run into different problems while using a web application. Having great customer service can be an advantage, especially if an investor is not tech-savvy.

- *Option to Trade Derivatives*

Unlike the stock market, the cryptocurrency market doesn't place much emphasis on derivatives such as options and futures. Nevertheless, these derivatives are used as a risk management strategy by many investors. A good crypto exchange provides the ability to trade these derivatives.

Decentralized Crypto Exchanges (DCEs)

There is no middleman while using decentralized crypto exchanges. All the exchanges happen directly between the seller and the buyer. However, the unpopularity of DCEs is because of the low liquidity. Even though they offer high security, they are still not popular among investors.

Understanding Bull and Bear Markets

Bull and bear markets are both terms used to explain market conditions. Investors typically choose one of these to proceed with their journey with either stock or cryptocurrency markets. The fundamental philosophical principles between bull and bear traders are also quite the opposite.

What is a Bull Market?

There is an increased demand for buying the assets in a bull market and a decreased rate of selling them. This makes crypto prices rocket and leads to economic booms. The bull market works well when there are announcements that show favorable prospects for a cryptocurrency. Most retail investors favor the bull market because the upward trend suggests that the companies behind these cryptocurrencies can generate more capital to create path-breaking changes.

What is a Bear Market?

There is a higher rate of selling assets in a bear market and a lower rate of buying them. Bear markets indicate a downward trend that can affect the economy. Many bears in the cryptocurrency market are big players and can change the market's sentiment by dumping their coins aggressively. Bear markets can lead to unfavorable economic outcomes such as unemployment.

What Should I Choose?

Choosing whether to be a bull or bear is an entirely personal preference based on how you feel about the market. Make sure that you try both of them and find out which you enjoy the most. Both bears and bulls are essential for the balance of the cryptocurrency market.

Understanding Options and Futures in the Cryptocurrency Market

Options and futures are known as derivatives. Derivatives depend entirely on assets such as stocks or cryptocurrencies to determine their value. Unlike stocks, the demand for derivatives in cryptocurrency markets is limited as it is difficult to bet on the crypto market due to its volatility and unpredictability.

What are futures?

When you buy a futures contract, you are betting that the price will either go up or down. You need to deliver the assets that you have said in the contract before the expiration date without a problem.

What are the options?

When you buy an options contract, you are buying a right to buy or sell a cryptocurrency at a particular price. However, you will not be obligated to exercise the options contract.

Are derivatives important for crypto enthusiasts?

Derivatives in the cryptocurrency market are difficult to estimate. However, with solid research and technical analysis, an investor can use derivatives to minimize losses as a risk management strategy.

Some Principles That Cryptocurrency Investors Need to Be Aware of

While it is true that Bitcoin offers more than traditional banks, you also need to make a considerable effort to understand what happens when you either send or receive a transaction. It would be best if you were extra careful sometimes to secure your cryptocurrency. This section will mention some of the essential principles that all cryptocurrency investors need to know.

Always Be Extra Careful About Your Wallet Information

Bitcoin has a private key and a public key that investors need to know. Whenever you request or send Bitcoins, the transaction uses your public key. You, however, will have a private key to open your Bitcoin wallet. It is just like a password for your social media accounts or e-mail. Remember that if you lose your wallet information, there will be no way to access your Bitcoins.

If you forget or lose your bank information, then there's a chance to reset them if you can visit a bank branch or portal. However, as Bitcoin is decentralized money, there is no way to access your wallet once you forget your public or private key. So, be extra careful.

Be Aware That Bitcoin Prices Will Fluctuate Heavily

Cryptocurrency is currently the most volatile financial instrument in the market. There are thousands of investors rallying around the blockchain revolution. Still, volatility exists because there are many traders and big players constantly pumping and dumping the coins to change the price of the cryptocurrency.

This volatility creates an inherent risk for investors and can make you lose your funds instantly. Also, as cryptocurrency is traded 24 hours a day, unlike stocks, you need to be extra aware of price changes. Never invest in cryptocurrencies with your monthly income. Always invest in cryptocurrencies with money from a savings account. We are not saying that you cannot create a steady income with cryptocurrencies, but it needs a lot of hard work and experience.

Remember That Bitcoin Transactions Are Irreversible

Cryptocurrencies run on trust. For example, let us suppose that you have visited the dark web to buy LSD or another drug that is banned in your country. Almost all shady web vendors are now using cryptocurrencies to manage transactions.

You find a website that will deliver that LSD to your shipping address for a given price. You pay using Bitcoin because you trust that vendor. However, even after a month, you still haven't received the LSD, and you now understand that you fell victim to a scam.

If these scams occur on digital platforms such as PayPal or Payoneer, you can flag the transaction for scam or fraud to get a refund. However, with Bitcoins, there is no way that you can receive a refund. All Bitcoin transactions are irreversible.

Understand Anonymity in Bitcoin Transactions

Almost no cryptocurrencies offer you privacy. All your transactions will be entered in a public ledger, and anyone can see them. However, almost all cryptocurrencies offer you anonymity. There is no way to link a Bitcoin wallet to your identity.

You should be careful not to reveal this sensitive information to anyone if you are worried about your anonymity. There are new cryptocurrencies that are being developed to provide you both privacy and anonymity.

Be Careful With Instant Transactions

Any blockchain specialist knows that it takes close to 10minutes to make a Bitcoin transaction. This short time frame can lead to many scams as the payee can stop the trade after sending a message to you. To avoid future headaches, make sure that you wait for at least 10 minutes to confirm the status of your transaction. You can use Litecoin to reduce the time of the transaction to 2.5 minutes.

The success of Bitcoin has made a lot of retail investors choose crypto. While Bitcoin has its merits, it has both scalability and interoperability issues, which have resulted in the creation of various other alternate cryptocurrencies with definite goals. Learning about these alternative cryptocurrencies can help a crypto investor to diversify their portfolio and be safe in a volatile market.

Chapter 5: Beyond Bitcoin Investing

Altcoins are cryptocurrency coins other than Bitcoin. They are in huge demand now because they cost less and yield high returns in less time than Bitcoin. Bitcoin is a popular cryptocurrency that drove the world into blockchain technology. However, from an investor's perspective, there is always a lot of room for other cryptocurrencies. Individuals should look at different cryptocurrencies that promise various features that Bitcoin cannot offer. Investing beyond Bitcoin is necessary for investors, especially when many blockchain developers are working hard to create a decentralized economy.

In this chapter, we will be discussing four alternative crypto coins that are popular and can be good choices for a beginner to invest in. They are Ethereum, Litecoin, Polkadot, and Cardano.

Understanding Ethereum and Its Importance

Any cryptocurrency enthusiast should have heard the name Ethereum at least once. It is presently the second most popular cryptocurrency, next to Bitcoin. Even with its popularity in crypto circles, many beginners are still not aware of Ethereum's goal and its impact on the cryptocurrency market. To know more about Ethereum, we need to address the importance of decentralized currency in this digital world.

Before the emergence of Bitcoin, many online/ digital transactions used to happen only with the help of official institutions such as banks. All digital alternatives such as PayPal also needed a bank account to withdraw your money. Simply put, people's transactions were being controlled and monitored by various authorities. In 2008, Bitcoin came into the picture with its innovative idea of making a decentralized system. People rallied around it, and it became an instant success.

Bitcoin may be extremely popular, but it also has a lot of inconveniences and limitations, which become more apparent as the platform ages and new, innovative platforms emerge.

The creators of Ethereum thought a step ahead and proposed different ways to use blockchain technology and its fundamental concept of decentralization to help address issues such as personal identification and verification of supply chains.

Why Can't We Use Bitcoin to Decentralize Other Institutions?

Blockchain requires an extensive network of computers to work, and during the initial stages of the cryptocurrency boom, Bitcoin was the only platform capable of decentralization. However, Bitcoin's features are minimal, and its programming language is challenging for programmers to use. These problems spurred Vitalik Buterin to develop Ethereum. He proposed the concept in 2014, and it has been considered a groundbreaker ever since in the crypto world.

What Is Ethereum Capable of?

The reason Ethereum was developed is to create decentralized programs based on blockchain. Because of the characteristics of blockchain, any program that has been created cannot be altered or changed by anyone else. All these programs are collectively known as DApps in the Ethereum platform.

To develop your own DApp, all you need to do is create it using Ethereum using their programming language known as Solidity.

Goals of Ethereum

Ethereum's only goal is to eliminate intermediaries on the Internet and create a decentralized Internet. The Internet is controlled by a few big companies nowadays, and Ethereum wants to get rid of these middlemen and help people connect without any hurdles.

For example, your hosting providers collect a lot of your data and use that information or sell it to other advertisers. Even multinational companies such as Facebook mine your data to change both your behavioral and psychological patterns. Ethereum's ultimate goal is to eliminate this advantage that tech giants have.

With Ethereum, an individual can create their services and sell them to others using its platform.

How Does Ethereum Work?

Ethereum's goals are revolutionary, and as an investor, you should be aware of certain things to precisely understand how it operates. Ethereum supports DApps function because of smart contracts. All these smart contracts are written in Solidity language.

Smart contracts are like a bunch of conditional statements that are necessary for a program to work. When a smart contract is placed in the Ethereum blockchain, it cannot be changed or altered. All the conditions will be executed by the blockchain whenever they are met.

This sounds intelligent and revolutionary, but even with all these advantages, some Bitcoin enthusiasts still consider Ethereum risky because there is no regulatory authority. This means it is an easy way for scammers to steal money from retail investors.

We will explain the infamous DAO attack in the next section to help you understand the different downsides of this concept.

DAO Attack and How It Shaped Ethereum

DAO stands for Decentralized Autonomous Organization. In 2016, it was the first DApp that came into operation over the Ethereum blockchain. What DAO essentially does is take votes from those who have invested in ICO funding to decide what the money should be used for. Over a few weeks, a whopping sum of 150 million dollars was collected to support the project.

However, after a few weeks, an attacker exploited a vulnerability in the DApp's code and stole nearly a third of the collected ethers. This lowered the value of Ethereum, and many investors claimed that the concept of Ethereum could not work if there was a way to steal money using the vulnerabilities present in the code.

The founder of Ethereum has taken this issue seriously and introduced several complex rules to bring back the trust. In the five years after this incident, Ethereum has successfully helped developers provide a platform where they can create decentralized apps that have a lot of potential to change both the Internet and the world.

Understanding Ether

While Ethereum is a platform to create DApps, all the computers in the network still need to spend a lot of energy and money to execute the contracts present in the blockchain. To make this happen, the authors of smart contracts pay using ethers. Whenever a smart contract is executed, ether will be exchanged in the blockchain.

Whenever you see the price change of the Ethereum blockchain, what that is referring to is the price of ether.

The Future of Ethereum

When Ethereum was first announced, there was a lot of hype due to its goal to make blockchain more powerful. It started to trade at 40 cents per coin and has risen remarkably over the years. As of this writing, Ethereum is at $3900 and still has great potential to grow in the next couple of years as there is a lot of opportunity for this cryptocurrency to change the world in a meaningful way.

Understanding Litecoin and Its Importance

Bitcoin was revolutionary and has created a path for different cryptocurrencies to emerge. As Bitcoin is open source, a lot of cryptocurrency enthusiasts have spent their time making it better. One project that has grown popular over time is Litecoin.

Litecoin's goal was never to replace Bitcoin. It is a project that was developed for Bitcoin enthusiasts to improve specific areas that Bitcoin falls short in.

Understanding Litecoin

Litecoin was released in 2011 as a knockoff of Bitcoin. Bitcoin is an open-source project. Hence, before Litecoin, many cryptocurrency coins based on Bitcoin had been developed. However, Litecoin won the race among them because it is easy to use and has a high transaction speed that Bitcoin lacks.

The mining speed is reduced from 10 minutes in Bitcoin to 2.5 minutes in Litecoin. It also offers more blocks than Bitcoin offers and uses a newer mining algorithm known as Scrypt for its users.

The advantage of Scrypt is that miners can use it in the standard graphics card desktops that most computer owners have. Bitcoin mining has become challenging to do on these regular desktops. Thus, many miners have migrated to heavy equipment that is generally used only for mining. Litecoin's goal is to help average desktop miners by providing an easy way to start mining and earn rewards.

Litecoin as Digital Silver

The popularity of Litecoin has increased over time and the currency is now called "digital silver." Bitcoin is still referred to as "digital gold" for revolutionizing blockchain and making the world walk along the path of decentralization.

Differences Between Litecoin and Bitcoin

As a popular knockoff cryptocurrency, there are a lot of similarities between Litecoin and Bitcoin. It is indeed essential to understand the differences that make both of them unique.

Transaction Time

The significant difference between Bitcoin and Litecoin is the time it takes to validate the currency. For huge transactions, Bitcoin is preferred by investors around the world. However, for urgent transactions, Litecoin is preferred because the transactions process four times faster.

Mining

Both Bitcoin and Litecoin use a proof of work algorithm to mine. However, Bitcoin makes miners work harder over time, and now all Bitcoin miners are forced to use ASIC equipment to validate transactions. It takes more energy and power to mine a block, which has allowed other methods such as proof of stake to emerge.

Litecoin uses the Scrypt algorithm to mine. It is fast and supports various graphic cards and regular desktops.

Can I Invest in Litecoin?

There is a lot of scope for Litecoin as an investment choice. Bitcoin is rallying in 2021, and this has led to investors choosing Litecoin for various reasons mentioned above. It is a better investment choice for cryptocurrency enthusiasts. The Litecoin community is terrific, and its founder is also a regular visitor of different cryptocurrency meetups worldwide.

Polkadot and its Importance

Polkadot has been dubbed the "Internet of blockchains" as it was created primarily to achieve blockchain communication. Polkadot and Cardano are the only two cryptocurrencies currently providing ways to make blockchain communication possible for developers, startups, and enterprises.

Why Blockchain Communication is Necessary

There are various popular cryptocurrencies such as Bitcoin, Ethereum, Litecoin, and XRP. All these, however, are isolated blockchains and cannot interact with each other in any way. Blockchain communication is necessary for making all blockchain applications interact with real-world users.

Ethereum is a famous blockchain platform that provides smart contracts for developers to create decentralized apps. With Polkadot, you can make a Bitcoin transaction that is otherwise impossible while using an Ethereum based decentralized application. Communication between blockchains can bring about a lot of other innovations.

The main reason blockchain platforms are not currently used by developers to create real-world accessible applications is because an increase in transactions will create bottlenecks that can delay the transaction time. A platform needs to be developed to have secure and reliable blockchain communication, but such a platform would have less scalability and some security issues.

Polkadot was developed to solve this problem. It uses a component known as the Polkadot Relay Chain to hold everything together and create a communication path between different isolated blockchains.

Understanding How Polkadot Works

All the blockchains in the network will be connected as spokes in the relay chain. This creates an easy way to communicate with different decentralized platforms or applications that exist in the network. All the blockchain networks that are present in the relay chain are known as parachains.

Polkadot also provides different ways to exchange data between chains. Information such as the account details, wallet details, and price of a security can be easily exchanged using Polkadot's relay chain protocol.

All these capabilities can help developers create applications that can constantly interact with different chains. It is a reliable way to develop complex apps that require a lot of data and a large user base.

Voting in Polkadot

Polkadot is also very well known for its interoperability. A lot of blockchains are controlled by companies and individuals, and any decentralized system needs to have a voting system to be transparent and trustworthy to all the stockholders that are involved.

Polkadot provides an exclusive feature by which all the stakeholders can vote during issues or while making upgrades. This is an excellent way to make sure everyone in the network or a blockchain is represented.

Upgrades in Polkadot

Many cryptocurrencies are made in such a way that the upgrades are challenging to execute. When a platform needs an upgrade, there is usually a hard fork. A hard fork changes the blockchain code and either introduces or deletes features and essentially creates a separate blockchain. Hard forking is extremely difficult in classic cryptocurrencies such as Bitcoin and Ethereum. Polkadot provides an easy way to make upgrades without making hard forks and dividing the community two.

Bridges in Polkadot

Polkadot uses bridges to communicate with isolated and independent blockchains such as Ethereum. Using bridges can allow instant communication between these isolated blockchains.

Should I Invest in Polkadot?

Polkadot helps developers and has a lot of potential. To make a decision, you need to understand Cardano, which does most of the things that Polkadot does. It is an intelligent decision to invest in Polkadot right now, as many developers are working hard to make blockchain accessible for real-world use. There is a lot of future potential for this blockchain platform.

Understanding Cardano and Its Importance

Cardano is a popular cryptocurrency that garnered attention because of its energy efficiency while mining. Bitcoin mining needs a lot of energy to validate all the transactions that happen in a blockchain, which leads to high coal consumption. While investors claim that more than 75% of Bitcoin miners use renewable energy sources, the environmental impact is still debated in crypto circles. In this section, we will provide detailed information about Cardano and how it functions.

Why Is Cardano Suddenly Popular?

Cardano has existed for quite some time. It has been available since September 2017, and since then, it has slowly gained traction with many crypto investors. It claims to solve a lot of problems that currently isolated blockchains are facing. However, even with many promises from its founder, it still hadn't gotten the attention it deserved until recently because many investors felt that Cardano's goals were nearly impossible to achieve.

Cardano gained attention with the publication of its whitepaper. Usually, whitepapers are published to announce a blockchain and its functionalities. Cardano's team, however, used an entirely new approach to explain what they were capable of. They verified their whitepaper with hundreds of researchers from all over the world and took suggestions from them. Thus, Cardano has become a peer-reviewed cryptocurrency even before its launch.

Cardano also claims to be a newer generation of blockchain cryptocurrencies. The first generation consists of Bitcoin, which was designed only to be used as digital gold. In the second generation, blockchain platforms such as Ethereum emerged to implement smart contracts and create decentralized apps that can change how the world interacts with cryptocurrencies. The next-generation cryptocurrencies such as Cardano use the best features of the previous generations and combine them to create something remarkable.

Why is Cardano the next Big Thing?

Cardano is considered the next big thing in the crypto world because it is designed to solve scalability and interoperability issues that affect first- and second-generation cryptocurrencies. We will explain some of these issues for your better understanding.

Solving Scalability Issues

Bitcoin suffers from scalability issues because when it was created, the code used proof of work as its verification method. Proof of work is tricky and consumes a lot of energy and power in the process.

Cardano uses a new technology known as proof of stake to validate transactions to counter this problem.

What is proof of stake?

With the proof of stake method, instead of everyone mining the blocks, the system restricts mining to just a few nodes known as slot leaders.

Cardano uses a time interval known as an 'epoch' to mine a block. There are many epochs, and each is given a slot leader, and they can mine only at that particular time. Cardano can increase scalability by adding several epochs for a block to decrease the transaction time. This method is very innovative and can do wonders in the next couple of years when people look for alternatives to Bitcoin due to its high energy consumption. Right now, all the power used for cryptocurrency mining in a year can power the whole of New Zealand for a year.

Network bandwidth is also a scalability issue that Cardano has solved with its new peer-to-peer technology. Usually, in a blockchain, all the computers in the network are interconnected and store all the transactions in the blockchain. With an increase in transactions, the network bandwidth needs to be increased, creating a scalability issue.

Cardano's founders solved this by creating subnetworks instead of putting all nodes in a single network. Cardano also created ways to interact with different nodes in subnetworks using a separate protocol similar to TCP/IP used for Internet communication.

Solving Interoperability Issues

All cryptocurrencies are currently independent and isolated. There is no way to convert your Bitcoin to Ethereum directly. You can do it, as mentioned earlier, using third parties, but it cuts out a chunk of the money in the form of transaction fees.

Cryptocurrency is currently booming, and within the next few years, there will be many cryptocurrencies. Cardano developers are constantly working to make it a chain of blockchains. Their ultimate goal is to make Cardano interact with any cryptocurrency that exists. This may take some time but has a lot of potential even in the early stages.

Cardano developers are also trying to make crypto transactions more like bank transactions so that the sender can understand details such as why and how currency is sent. However, remember that this is only an optional feature, and you don't have to use it if you prefer not to. Entering metadata can help you organize or utilize your transactions effectively.

How Can Cardano Sustain Itself in the Long run?

Cardano is thinking of various ways to maintain itself in the long run. For example, it uses a treasury system to support the currency and its platform and make any significant changes to the platform.

How Does the Treasury Work?

For every transaction you do in the network, a small percentage will be sent to the treasury. The money sent to the treasury will be released only when there are approved proposals by the community.

The basic process is like this :

1. Developers make their proposals and submit or post them in the community, detailing all the improvements they wish to make.

2. Then, all the members in the community vote for different proposals that have been submitted, and whoever wins the vote will be sent money to continue with the project.

3. After the project is completed, the Cardano team will check it thoroughly for any security or scalability issues. If there are no problems, then the Cardano team will deploy the upgrade into the blockchain.

Should I Invest in Cardano?

Right now, Cardano is a popular crypto coin, especially for beginners. It is still trading at a low price, making it an easy investment for those with less capital. Cardano is also reliable to invest in because it uses less power and energy.

Ethereum, Litecoin, Polkadot, and Cardano are currently considered an investor's best choice for investment due to the features they provide. There are fortunately several other alternative cryptocurrencies that may be worth a try for an ambitious crypto investor.

Chapter 6: More Alternative Crypto Coins

It is often difficult to research and judge the value of altcoins because outside of whitepapers, it can be difficult to find trustworthy sources that discuss blockchains. A lot of cryptocurrency enthusiasts recommend beginners start investing in altcoins to earn higher profits than they would with Bitcoin. This chapter will present some of the popular altcoins with a detailed discussion about them. Why is it important to look at other cryptocurrencies?

Some Bitcoin enthusiasts insist that Bitcoin is the only cryptocurrency that can truly thrive. However, a lot of cryptocurrency investors believe that all these altcoins have as much potential as Bitcoin. The reason for the increase in this sentiment was the tremendous success of the Ethereum blockchain platform.

It is now the second most popular cryptocurrency in terms of both price and market capitalization. Many innovative decentralized apps are being developed using Ethereum, and the latest trend of purchasing NFTs is also possible through Ethereum.

Different blockchain platforms are being developed to cover the drawbacks that Bitcoin comes with. Even though it has been a popular and impactful currency thus far, Bitcoin has a lot of flaws. For example, the proof of work mechanism consumes a lot of power and energy and is overall a bad use of renewable energy sources such as coal. Alternative cryptocurrencies find solutions for these problems and provide innovative mechanisms to utilize the power of blockchain.

How to Judge an Alternative Cryptocurrency

Anyone can make a cryptocurrency easily. All you need is some programming experience and a bunch of time. However, to create effective blockchain platforms, you need to be dedicated and spend your time wisely to make everything work. As an investor, the ability to judge whether a cryptocurrency works is an important skill. There are several ways to build this skill.

1. Read a lot about cryptocurrency.

2. Study a cryptocurrency's whitepaper to learn about the platform's goals and plans.

3. Research currencies' founders and their technical abilities to decide whether they can deliver what they intend to.

4. Participate in communities and forums, and talk about various features that you like or that seem problematic. In the initial stages, even creators of a cryptocurrency will reach out to you to help you understand their coin's philosophy.

5. Always do a thorough fundamental analysis to judge the value of a cryptocurrency.

6. Understand each currency's security mechanism and whether it is green crypto that consumes less power and energy.

The future of cryptocurrency is very bright. As an investor, you need to diversify your bag (portfolio) with several altcoins to avoid the effects of a steep decrease in a single cryptocurrency's value. Fortunately, there are quite a few good altcoin investments you can make.

10 Popular Cryptocurrencies that Investors Need to Be Aware of

To make this list, we have considered factors such as market capitalization, the future outlook, community activity, and innovative ideas to popularize the blockchain platform.

1. Stellar (XLM)

Stellar is a popular third-generation cryptocurrency whose main goal is to increase transaction speed and improve scalability. It also charges a very low transaction fee to the user. Stellar has been an underappreciated cryptocurrency for years even with its excellent energy efficiency mining protocols. Stellar is at its core a distributed ledger technology that can offer seamless payments for users in the network.

When the Stellar blockchain was introduced, the company controlling it released a fixed sum of 100 billion lumens, cryptocurrency in the Stellar blockchain platform. It uses the SCP protocol to effectively add confirmed transactions to the distributed ledger.

How Stellar Works

Stellar acts as an anchor between two banks. These isolated banks are connected using a Stellar network and can help easily transfer money between two banks within seconds. Usually, with fiat currency, foreign transactions take at least 2 days to arrive.

Let's say Sarah lives in the UK and Mark lives in the US. Sarah decides to send 350 British pounds (GBP) to Mark. Now, usually, it is difficult to send the money because their banks are in different countries, and they may use different technologies and protocols.

Instead of going through the banks, Sarah's debited money gets sent to the Stellar network where the currency is converted to XLM and is sent to the US. Then, the Stellar network finds the best exchange rates to convert XLM to USD. After that, the money will be credited to Mark's account. This is exactly how Stellar and its cryptocurrency XLM introduced seamless real-world transactions using blockchain.

The Stellar blockchain platform provides various bank-related services such as P2P lending, micro-insurance, and conditional cash transfers. It is a very revolutionary idea and has a lot of potential for gaining profits in the future. It can also be considered green crypto since it consumes very little energy.

Should I Invest in Stellar?

It's a solid investment choice. A lot of investors in the Stellar community have been disappointed because there is no expected profit for a few years. However, in 2021, it is gaining attention, and we are sure that a lot of investors are going to pour into it after learning its advantages over other cryptocurrencies.

2. Tether

Tether is a popular Stablecoin right now in the cryptocurrency market. Stablecoins are used when there is high volatility in the market. Stablecoins are also popular because they have a higher liquidity rate and are easy to start with.

Stablecoins are a type of cryptocurrency that was developed to reduce the gap that exists between fiat currency and cryptocurrency. Tether's value is always equal to 1 US dollar and even when there are short price fluctuations, the company that controls Tether pushes the price of Tether to $1 using their currency reserves.

Why are Stablecoins Such as Tether Used?

The main reason Stablecoins are used is to quickly liquidate the cryptocurrencies such as Bitcoin or Ethereum to a currency that is equal to fiat currency. You can liquidate Bitcoins or ethers to the fiat currency of your choice using a Bitcoin exchange, but it can take a lot of time and the transaction fees will be higher.

Tether is right now used in many blockchains such as Ethereum, Algorand, and TRON. It is presently one of the most popular cryptocurrencies in terms of market capitalization and cryptocurrency with the highest day trading volume.

Should I Invest in Tether?

It is a smart investment move to have reserves of Tether in your portfolio. You can quickly exchange them for any other cryptocurrency without handling high transaction fees. You can purchase Tether using regular blockchain wallets such as Binance and then you can use them to liquidate during sudden market swings.

The ticker symbol of Tether is USDT. As a crypto investor, you may have doubts about the reserves that are available, but you need not worry because the founders of Tether mentioned that they use money from various sources to help crypto investors reduce the gap between fiat and digital currency.

3. Chainlink

Chainlink has received a great response from cryptocurrency circles over the past two years. Chainlink became many crypto investors' favorite because it solves an essential problem for the smart contract ecosystem. Smart contracts are an innovation in blockchains and were first used in Ethereum. Later they were adapted to various blockchain platforms to create decentralized applications that can change the world.

What smart contracts do is automatically execute actions and events when particular pre-written terms happen. They are just lines of code but can independently work without anyone's interference in the blockchain. However, as of now, the applications of smart contracts are quite limited because they can't access data feeds.

Chainlink's Purpose

The idea and implementation of Chainlink are considered revolutionary; they trigger smart contracts depending on the real-world events that are collected from data feeds all over the world. For example, you can create smart contracts to trigger an event when climate changes in Mississippi. There are unlimited possibilities that smart contracts can generate now using these data feeds.

Chainlink gets data from data providers known as oracles. Oracles follow a decentralized system and are not controlled by anyone. They provide reliable data and earn rewards in the blockchain cryptocurrency LINK token. They will also be penalized if they send wrong or inaccurate information.

Now, when blockchain technology becomes more intense there will be thousands of smart contracts running. All these smart contracts can utilize data providers such as Chainlink to improve their services.

There are however some controversies that surround this crypto coin. Many believe that a lot of coins in this blockchain are controlled by a few big players and this makes Chainlink a centralized service. Despite these claims, the founders have remarked that they are being transparent.

Should I Invest in Chainlink?

Chainlink was created because there is a demand for using reliable data for smart contracts. Chainlink acts as one decentralized API pool for cryptocurrency programmers and businesses. Over time, when smart contracts and decentralized applications increase, there will be a lot of demand for Chainlink. The ticker symbol for Chainlink is LINK.

4. Uniswap

There is recently a lot of hype around the Uniswap blockchain at the moment. Simply put, its main purpose is to exchange or swap decentralized tokens in the Ethereum blockchain. The primary goal around decentralized exchanges is that they are different from centralized exchanges when it comes to transaction fees, time, and especially liquidity. Ten years into the successful blockchain revolution, there are lesser-known exchanges that can compete with centralized ones.

How Uniswap Works

The original idea behind Uniswap was first proposed by the founder of Ethereum, but many thought that it would be practically impossible to implement it until the founder of Uniswap did it.

Uniswap uses something known as an automated market maker. Using automated market maker protocol, Ethereum smart contracts automatically interact with liquidity pools when there is a transaction request.

Liquidity pools have liquidity providers that provide both Ethereum and stablecoin tokens such as USDT. This is like using a stake to work. When there is a need for a transaction for 1ETH, the Uniswap algorithm will first convert it into stablecoins and will use ether to exchange the tokens. This is not only effective but also happens seamlessly.

Should I Invest in Uniswap?

Uniswap is now a high-demand cryptocurrency due to the rise in NFTs. Non-fungible tokens are a way to buy non-replaceable digital tokens for a particular piece of art and a lot of NFTs use protocols such as Uniswap to exchange or swap.

Uniswap also will provide a way to lend your current stake in coins to liquidity providers. This is also considered a safe investment because you will get a lending fee as a reward. UNI is the ticker symbol for this cryptocurrency token.

5. The Graph

The Graph is being called the Google of blockchains because it provides a logical and reasonable solution to the problem of indexing in decentralized applications. It is available exclusively for the Ethereum blockchain and uses Graph QL technology to query the relevant data in the blockchain.

Why Is The Graph Necessary?

The Graph is necessary because Ethereum's decentralized applications usually have difficulty interacting with the data that is already stored in the blockchain. This drawback made developers spend extra time or create their own spreadsheets to carefully analyze data. The Graph is a decentralized algorithm that offers a solution to this problem.

How The Graph Works

Usually, all the data that is entered in the blockchain is sent into the nodes and is made available to decentralized application developers. With The Graph, however, Graph QL becomes a bridge between the data and the applications that need them. It provides a route for this data to flow easily.

It takes a lot of people in the network to complete the tasks. For example, consumers in the network successfully verify the indexes that are being queried and members known as arbitrators will check if there is any malicious intent behind the request.

Should I Invest in The Graph?

The Graph is a demanding service that is essential for decentralized applications to work effectively. You can compare it to a database management system for websites, but it works in a more powerful and non-regulatory manner. When people start to build more decentralized applications and query more data, then the demand for this cryptocurrency will increase exponentially. It is a smart investment, and its ticker symbol is GRT in the crypto exchanges.

6. EOS

Ethereum has changed the dynamics of blockchain platforms and technology by introducing smart contracts. However, Ethereum had scalability issues and a lot of app developers faced problems deploying working applications in the blockchain. To counter this problem, in 2017 EOS blockchain was introduced. It was called an alternative for Ethereum, but even after several years, it still hasn't gotten the attention it deserves.

How EOS Works

EOS can be used by developers to create decentralized applications. EOS has very few scalability issues and authenticates users with its native tokens. It also allows application developers to easily upgrade their applications without causing any problems for its user base. It is also extremely flexible compared to other smart contract blockchain platforms. Its ticker symbol is also EOS.

Should I Invest in EOS?

It is a promising alternative cryptocurrency that is very useful for smart contract application developers. EOS is also more decentralized than Ethereum and is transparent about all its governance and interoperability issues. In 2021, EOS is a promising investment choice.

7. Aave

Decentralized finance's goal is to create a financial system that is entirely independent of the centralized finance systems that we are used to. It is a groundbreaking phenomenon and has the potential to change the world.

Ethereum platform needs lending pools to make decentralized exchange transactions, and cryptocurrencies like Aave are a good choice for this purpose. It can be used to provide flash loans to users in the network for a provided stake.

Should I Invest in Aave?

With the Ethereum blockchain platform's rise in popularity, Aave has great long-term potential. It still has very little market capitalization because it is still relatively new, but it can help investors gain huge returns in the coming years.

8. Algorand

The problem with a lot of cryptocurrencies is that they expect to work and solve only one problem. While Bitcoin is regarded as digital gold, it has very limited capabilities and has scalability issues. Ethereum, on the other hand, started the concept of smart contracts but has issues with speed.

Algorand is a blockchain platform that was created to counter all these problems at once and create a decentralized platform that has high speed, very few scalability issues, and a lot of value. Its ticker symbol is ALGO.

How Algorand Works

Algorand uses a proof of stake mechanism to validate the transactions. Algorand uses energy-efficient techniques to mine the blocks that are inserted in the blockchain. Algorand also divides its protocol based on smart contracts. It supports both basic and advanced smart contracts. The first layer is mostly used for simple proof of chain smart contracts and the second layer of the Algorand protocol is used for more robust and demanding decentralized applications.

Should I invest in Algorand?

Algorand has a lot of potential and yielded more than 200% returns over the past year for investors. It is an interesting project with a supportive community. Algorand is a solid choice for long-term investment. However, it may have short-term price fluctuations and if you are a day trader, then we recommend you do not solely depend on Algorand as an investment choice.

9. Tezos

Energy and power consumption are a problem for most cryptocurrencies. This issue has spurred startups to create cryptocurrencies that use proof of stake technology instead of proof of work. Tezos is a proof of stake coin and offers a lot of opportunities for investors who are investing in green cryptocurrencies. Its ticker symbol is XTZ in cryptocurrency exchanges.

Why is Tezos revolutionary?

Apart from its revolutionary proof of stake mechanism, it also supports self-amending protocols to upgrade regularly without being affected by hard forks.

Another reason Tezos is revolutionary is that it provides governance to the users in the network itself. Even with an aggressive bear attack for Tezos due to lawsuits, it has survived mainly because of its effective voting mechanism that allows the users in the network to make decisions. With growing concern over the Bitcoin and Ethereum networks' energy issues, this could be a good alternative blockchain platform that may bring profits to investors.

Should I invest in Tezos?

Tezos also supports the creation of smart contracts and decentralized applications using the blockchain platform. This can be a good investment choice if you are aware of the concerns that popular cryptocurrencies face. However, we recommend you don't make it a huge part of your portfolio because it is considered an extremely volatile cryptocurrency.

10.Dogecoin

Dogecoin is a cryptocurrency that has recently gained massive popularity, and the funny thing is it is a meme coin. Meme coins are a group of coins that became recently popular because of Tesla CEO Elon Musk's tweets. Musk has endorsed this cryptocurrency and made its price skyrocket. It is now a popular cryptocurrency and is gaining a lot of hype and love from retail investors around the Internet.

What Are Dogecoin's Features?

Technically, it is just a normal blockchain technology but uses much more efficient ways to mine blocks and has an unlimited supply of coins. This, however, can be a bad value in the future because high inflation can be a problem. The success of decentralized currencies such as Bitcoin is mainly because they are limited.

Dogecoin uses the Scrypt algorithm to mine and is quite similar to Litecoin from a technical standpoint. Even with all these efficiencies, Dogecoin is still primarily a cryptocurrency that was made for fun. The founder of the blockchain used a meme called "doge" for the name of the cryptocurrency. Incidentally, he made this cryptocurrency in just 2 hours.

Should I Invest in Dogecoin?

We will give a controversial opinion on this. Both investors and speculators bet on an asset because it provides value over years. They also constantly check companies' policies over time and understand what the companies are up to. Ethereum and its ecosystem have developed in this way.

Now, with Dogecoin there is no way to understand what its purpose is. There is no development or underlying goal that can make investors pump it forever. It is a high-risk investment because it is overvalued right now. You can invest in Dogecoin, but it can be extremely volatile and has the potential for quick losses. Be cautious.

Chapter 7: Cryptocurrency and the Future

In 2021 all cryptocurrencies are in a bullish mode. Investors have seen excellent returns with every coin from Bitcoin to the new evolving proof of stake coins such as Cardano and Polkadot. The ongoing pandemic has increased people's focus on blockchain technology in the future. In this chapter, we will discuss cryptocurrencies and their future outlook.

Is it Too Late for Me to Invest in Cryptocurrency?

With cryptocurrencies, people tend to ask many questions about whether they are a good investment choice. Institutional investors always have doubts before investing with brick-and-mortar companies. They do thorough research and decide whether something is a valuable asset.

When it comes to cryptocurrencies, people get confused looking at the prices. Many say that the reason they don't buy is that the price is too high for them. Recently, Bitcoin reached over $50,000, and

Ethereum has traded at prices upwards of $4,000. This is a lot of money for most people, and the prices are much higher than those of top stocks. However, you can buy a fraction of Bitcoin. The smallest amount of Bitcoin is Satoshi, and it is 1: 100,000,00 of Bitcoin.

Cryptocurrency is here to stay, and it is never too late to invest in it. The main reason it will never lose its value is because of its limited supply. When there is a limited supply, there always will be value.

Why isn't it too late to invest in cryptocurrencies?

Now Is the Time

2021 has been a great run for cryptocurrency enthusiasts. Bitcoin has tripled its value, and other altcoins have increased their value in similar manners. However, some people are worried that all this is a bubble and it will burst soon.

Be that as it may, we should remember the dot-com bust. This happened during the 2000s when people were investing in Internet-related stocks. Overnight, people lost a lot of money but did the Internet stop evolving? No. Right now, many high-valued tech companies are in some way linked to the Internet and provide services on it.

Like the Internet, blockchain is also an innovative technology that has a lot of potential to change the world, and it is always the right time to invest in it. In 2009, it was very easy to get Bitcoins, and after a few years, it became a phenomenon, and many people got into it. But after that, Bitcoin's price fell, and people doubted its longevity. Seven years later, they are still asking the same question. This is the time. It is always time to get on the cryptocurrency bandwagon.

Supply and Demand

The obvious reason it is never late to invest in cryptocurrency is that there is a very limited supply of Bitcoins. Only 21 million Bitcoins can be produced, and almost all cryptocurrencies use the same concept and produce only a limited supply of coins to combat inflation.

Normal centralized currency is always risky because the central banks can print as much money as possible and create a monetary risk for everyone involved. Almost all tech companies, governments, retail, and hedge funds are quickly entering the cryptocurrency game, and the limited supply will make the prices of these cryptocurrencies skyrocket. When there is demand, there will always be supply. That's a classic rookie tip.

Limited Supply Also Increases Value

What will happen when the limited number of crypto coins are mined? Will they lose their value? That is very unlikely to happen. Scarcity always increases demand, and the price of cryptocurrencies will rise over time rather than fall as many predict. Of course, there is always a problem with panic selling among investors. Still, with the ambition and research of cryptocurrency enthusiasts, we don't think there will be panic selling unless there are some serious reforms from governments to make cryptocurrency illegal.

Blockchain

Now, let's discuss the main reason that cryptocurrencies can never lose their value. It's definitely because of blockchain. The secure protocol that cryptocurrency depends on gives crypto a distinct advantage. Innovations are being made for its use in different areas and blockchain interaction with the help of technologies such as Polkadot.

People rally around blockchain technology because it can bring greater transparency in health, politics, and supply chain, to name a few.

The Power of Smart Contracts

Smart contracts are the talk of the town in crypto circles. In addition to creating DApps, smart contracts can also be used to store non-fungible tokens forever in the blockchain. We will be discussing NFTs in detail in the coming chapter.

All of these are reasons for you to start investing in cryptocurrencies. If you care about immediate high-profit returns, we suggest you look at the altcoins that we have discussed before. It's been just 12 years since Bitcoin was created. There is still a lot of hope for the future as investors expect that Bitcoin will reach 1 Million US dollars by 2030. Other cryptocurrencies that offer reliable ways to utilize blockchain technology effectively show similar promise.

Cryptocurrency as a Global Phenomenon

Bitcoin was popular among different parts of the world right from its invention. The market capitalization of Bitcoin is close to 1 trillion dollars now and is at this moment the 10th most valuable asset in the world.

Unlike tech companies traded only in one stock exchange, Bitcoin is available to anyone from any part of the world. The global phenomenon of cryptocurrency technology is often under-discussed for various reasons. In this section, we will talk about some of the countries that have the highest cryptocurrency holders.

The United States

Almost 8% of the United States population is now directly or indirectly invested in cryptocurrencies. A lot of them are very optimistic about the currency's performance. The United States government, however, is worried about the concept that cryptocurrencies were built upon. The IRS also mentioned to congress that people are investing in Bitcoin to avoid paying taxes.

Despite these controversies, many developers, startups, and companies hail from the United States.

Romania

Romania's economy is highly dependent on IT firms and domestic companies. Also, many people in Romania have tech jobs and are knowledgeable about cryptocurrencies. Obviously, because of this knowledge, Romania is said to hold the highest number of cryptocurrencies per capita. Almost 14% of the population in Romania has at least one crypto coin.

China

China has always been harsh on cryptocurrency investors. We can easily understand why a country that monitors its citizens constantly is afraid of cryptocurrency. To encourage people not to use cryptocurrency, China has made centralized digital currency easily available for citizens.

Companies like Alibaba and Tencent QQ provide wallet services that are fast, secure, and reliable. China's government knows that there is no way to stop individuals from buying or holding cryptocurrency, so they are developing the next wave of digital currency. For investors, there is always doubt about cryptocurrency's future in China.

Japan

Japan is one of the few countries that is pro-crypto. It encourages its citizens to make their payments using cryptocurrencies. Japan also holds the second highest market capitalization in cryptocurrencies after the United States. Japanese officials feel that cryptocurrency has a lot of potential and can change the world.

A separate regulatory authority exists for approving different blockchain technologies and virtual currencies.

South Korea

South Korea is a hub for tech companies and software engineers from around the world. It has a high-tech demographic that is extremely enthusiastic about crypto and its future. Many Chinese investors are also creating offshore accounts in South Korea because they fear their government may ban cryptocurrency.

More than 10% of all crypto trading volume is dependent on South Korean investors; thus, the country holds a large stake in a global phenomenon.

Switzerland

We all know that Switzerland is famous for its banking systems, and a lot of banks allow very high privacy for their depositors. This is the main reason there are a lot of international account holders in Swiss banking institutions.

However, even though its banking system is centralized, Swiss banks are very encouraging of the use of cryptocurrencies in their workflow. Switzerland is also home to a lot of tech companies and crypto enthusiasts.

Apart from these countries, Spain, France, Germany, India, and Egypt are also contributing to the cryptocurrency boom. All crypto investors, regardless of where they hail from, are extremely optimistic about its future.

Cryptocurrency's main goal is to be used in poor and backward countries. Right now, it is minimal in developing countries, and there are still a lot of ways to go to make this decentralization available in both corrupt and poor economies. For example, a few years back, when there was an increase in the huge inflation rate in Venezuela and their local currency decreased in value, several individuals started to use Bitcoin to make transactions.

Will Digital Currency Ever Die?

Cryptocurrency is a form of digital currency. All centralized bank transactions that happen online also fall under the digital currency category. Smart international deposit solutions such as PayPal and Payoneer are also a form of digital currency.

Will digital currency ever die? No. There is no way that the world could handle the death of digital currency because almost every business on the Internet uses digital transactions. If digital currency fails, all these businesses wouldn't be able to accept payment, and the economy would collapse.

As a cryptocurrency enthusiast, you need not worry about this problem because there is no chance of this happening anytime soon.

The Digital War Among the USA, China, and Russia

There are always downsides to any investment that has value. And when technologies like blockchain arise, governments closely observe them to find ways to disrupt other countries' economies.

Right now, The United States, China, and Russia are at war. Instead of fighting with jets and artillery like in the 20th century, these countries are now fighting digitally. As there is a lot at stake, there is also an ongoing war with the countries regarding cryptocurrency.

China is very strict on its citizens about using cryptocurrency. Over the years, it has placed several restrictions so people could not use digital gold as a valid decentralized currency. However, the vocal crypto community in China has made it quite impossible for their government to make it illegal altogether. Conversely, both the US and Russia are very welcoming to cryptocurrency technologies because they care about the ultimate power it gives their country.

Will this global war affect coin prices? It's highly unlikely because even though governments have a specific goal, it is very difficult to hack or steal cryptocurrencies from the blockchain. The only way this would become a problem is if these countries start to use cryptocurrencies to fund their wars, which is a real possibility.

Cryptocurrency and its future are very promising. All over the world, thousands of programmers are spending hours creating decentralized applications and platforms to make people interact more. The future of cryptocurrency is entirely dependent, at least for now, on the prowess of programmers, startups, and companies to make innovations and revolutionize the overall ecosystem it offers.

Chapter 8: Understanding Ripple and XRP ledger

Ripple is ambitious and has been a talk of the town for years within the crypto world. It has a native cryptocurrency token known as XRP and offers a payment network that runs on blockchain technology to make instantaneous transactions, similar to how information is sent and stored. Understanding the Ripple network, its cryptocurrency XRP, and its relation to the banking system is essential for any serious crypto investor.

Why Is Ripple Necessary?

Ripple was created because our present banking system takes a frustratingly long time to send money to foreign accounts. If you want to send to domestic accounts, it takes place within seconds because countries have developed efficient payment systems to make transactions seamless.

However, nothing has changed much in 40 years to make foreign transactions easier. There are services such as PayPal or Payoneer that have become popular for sending or receiving funds internationally. Even with these advanced payment platforms, it still takes 5-7 business days to reflect funds in your bank account. Another disadvantage is that banks regulate everything, and you need to pay hefty charges to withdraw your money.

Ripple is a blockchain-based project to make payments instantaneously all over the world within five to seven seconds.

Why Have Banks Failed for Years to Speed up Foreign Transactions?

Banks are lazy. They don't like to change a system that has been working for them for years. Let's now see what happens when you want to send money to a foreign account using your local bank.

1. You go to your bank's official website or sometimes directly to a bank branch to send $1000 to your vendor in Pakistan.

2. When you place a request to send money, your bank first checks your ledger to see whether you have sufficient money in your account. If you have a sufficient balance, then the money will be debited and sent to your client's bank account.

3. However, there is no way to send money directly to your client's account because they live in another country. The other country uses completely different regulations and technologies for digital or wire payments. So, the money is sent into the client's account using different intermediary banks. This procedure, however, takes a lot of time and can sometimes fail because of server issues.

4. In addition to waiting the long transaction time, the client also needs to pay an exchange fee for converting USD into their currency. This exchange fee is usually costly and can cut your profits over time.

This is what Ripple has promised to change. To make these transactions feasible and convenient, the developers of the Ripple network have created a protocol known as RTXP.

Understanding RippleNet

Ripple was first envisioned by its founder as a decentralized monetary system in which communities can generate their own money using the protocols that Ripple provides. The idea gathered immediate attention because at that time people were worried about the transaction times that Bitcoin and Ethereum had. Ripple founders came with a concept to easily transfer or hold money across borders within seconds. It was what all cryptocurrency enthusiasts had envisioned. Ripple was a favorite investment choice for many investors, and it is still going strong with the third highest market capitalization only after Bitcoin and Ethereum.

RippleNet is very reliable and guarantees that all the transactions will be processed within a few seconds. It also offers highly scalable operations and changed how people saw blockchain transaction speed when it was first introduced.

RippleNet follows a decentralized system using the XRP ledger blockchain mechanism. XRP is the native token of this ledger system. The XRP ledger has high security due to its advanced use of cryptographic algorithms to both secure and validate transactions.

The main difference between more popular cryptocurrencies such as Bitcoin or Ethereum and XRP is there is no concept of mining in RippleNet. This makes it an obvious choice for investors who care about power and energy consumption. It instead uses a separate node mechanism by which all the transactions are confirmed by certain validators. All these validator nodes are publicly available UNL nodes, which are official nodes that are usually used by banking systems around the globe.

Ripple is also popular with other financial institutions because it offers ways to fully tackle the problem with cryptocurrency scams such as money laundering. The Ripple team is constantly monitoring transactions and helps people not fall prey to scams.

You may call this is centralization, but RippleNet founders argue that providing a secure layer is never centralization.

Should I Invest in XRP?

XRP is used as a bridge payment network for foreign transactions. Having a native blockchain currency makes the transactions seamless on RippleNet and it was created with a maximum of 100 billion XRP in circulation. Most of them are locked in an escrow account and will only be released at a rate of a billion per month to avoid high inflation rates. This demonstrates that XRP is a safe investment and has transparent founders whose main goal is to achieve a decentralized monetary system that will altogether eliminate the need for centralized exchanges.

Pros and Cons of Ripple

It is important to understand both advantages and disadvantages a monetary system offers before starting to use it for any reason.

Pros

Excellent infrastructure

Ripple, which controls the circulation of XRP, has used its initial funding to create a robust infrastructure that can help it create fast and reliable transactions with few scalability issues.

High Demand

The popularity of XRP is due to its being heavily backed by big players in the industry. Many feel that it can be a bridge between fiat and cryptocurrency and can be logically used in real-world applications.

No inflation problem

Ripple founders have used the same concept Satoshi Nakamoto used to reduce the inflation that could arise if there were an unlimited supply. However, Ripple has a higher market cap than Bitcoin (100 billion vs. 21

million), which makes it affordable to beginners and investors with less capital.

Cons

Somewhat centralized

Unlike other cryptocurrencies, RippleNet involves banks and validators that are public nodes to validate the transactions. This removes the anonymity and privacy that decentralized financial institutions offer. However, Ripple founders have explained that the XRP ledger is secure and cannot be tampered with by any means.

Many competitors

Decentralized finance is now the hot topic among crypto circles and a lot of cryptocurrencies such as Stellar are being created to revolutionize decentralized monetary systems. Over time, all these cryptocurrencies will advance, and Ripple needs to make huge revolutionary advancements to stay in the game.

Chapter 9: Understanding NFTs & ICOs

This chapter will provide a detailed explanation of two crucial concepts that Cryptocurrency enthusiasts should be aware of. ICOs were part of the cryptocurrency world from the beginning, and they receive a lot of love and hate for different reasons. Then there are NFTs, the latest trend among crypto enthusiasts.

Understanding NFTs

Before talking about NFTs, we need to address value. Where does the value of a painting or an asset come from? What does value mean from a technical perspective?

Financially, value is something that grows over time. For example, Tesla shares have skyrocketed over the years, and it can be called a valuable stock. Similarly, Bitcoin can also be called a worthwhile investment.

Now, let us come back to the discussion of NFTs. NFT is the abbreviation for non-fungible token. These tokens cannot be replaced and are unique.

What is a Token?

A lot of people confuse coins and tokens. A coin is entirely dependent on the blockchain and thus can be considered native. For example, the Ethereum blockchain uses ether as its native coin. Every cryptocurrency blockchain has a coin that investors can use for exchanges.

Tokens, on the other hand, have a wide variety of uses including storing the intrinsic value of an asset or making a purchase. Tokens can be created in DApps to be used for particular purposes.

There are both fungible and non-fungible tokens on the Ethereum platform. Fungible tokens can be changed and are not unique, unlike non-fungible tokens. When someone owns a non-fungible token, they are the only valid owner of that asset even if multiple copies are on the open Internet. Owning a non-fungible token is like having rightful ownership of digital art.

Why Did NFTs Suddenly Become Popular?

Non-fungible tokens are available on the Ethereum blockchain platform as well as several others for obvious reasons such as popularity and scalability, many vendors or marketplaces where auctions take place use Ethereum supported NFTs.

In March 2021, Twitter CEO Jack Dorsey posted a tweet saying that he would auction his first tweet on Twitter as an NFT. Until then, even many crypto enthusiasts were unaware of the phenomenon of NFT that was starting to take the world by storm.

Sina Estavi, a famous entrepreneur, won the bid for the tweet for a whopping sum of 2.9 million dollars, to everyone's surprise. Can you believe it?

Non-fungible tokens are considered by many to be a raging phenomenon that makes no sense. But many digital artists and musicians are happy that they can sell their art directly to their audiences without paying a massive price to intermediaries. Right now, almost every art auction website takes roughly 20% of sales as processing and handling fees. With a blockchain platform, you can now purchase a token and can claim your rightful ownership to any media.

When Did NFTs First Appear?

NFTs go a long way back. But it became hyped when people started using an Ethereum based decentralized app known as CryptoKitties. In this app, users purchase virtual cats and own them forever because the blockchain generates a non-fungible token. CryptoKitties became so popular that Ethereum couldn't handle the overwhelming number of transactions.

With time, the CryptoKitties hype has vanished, but the concept of selling the ownership of digital art or media did not disappear. Right now, many marketplaces are selling and auctioning digital media as NFTs.

Why Should I Care About NFTs?

The concept of Non-fungible tokens is quite contradictory to Bitcoins, which can be exchanged and have the same value; they represent a whole different point of view cryptocurrency investors can concentrate on.

All real estate agencies quote a price for the house or a condo based on its value in the real world. In the same way, you can treat non-fungible tokens as digital assets that are priced based on their value. In the future, NFTs can be used to own an asset or for identity management.

Why Are NFTs Important?

NFTs are important because they provide an easy way for artists to sell their creations. If you care about your favorite artists getting the money they deserve, using NFTs is a good idea. NFTs are also crucial for an investor because you can buy and sell these assets when there is a considerable demand for an NFT.

The NBA has recently announced top shots, an NFT platform that allows users to own small clips of the top shots of a game. Many musical artists, film artists, and athletes will soon start selling their own NFTs.

How Do I Buy and Sell NFTs?

NFTs usually run on the Ethereum blockchain. To create a non-fungible token in an Ethereum blockchain, you need to pay a transaction fee in ether. As of now, you have to spend at least a few hundreds of dollars' worth of ether to start selling your NFTs in marketplaces around the Internet. This is a good process because all the marketplaces would otherwise be filled with people selling worthless media and content to make some quick bucks.

To buy NFT, all you need to do is place your bid, and if no one can place a bid higher than yours, then the NFT will be sent to you, and you will become the rightful owner of the asset.

How Can Investors Use NFTs?

You can trade NFTs and can sell them for a higher price to other interested people. Just like any real-world art that collectors can trade, NFTs can also be traded. However, you need to follow the market carefully and should understand the demand to supply ratio. There are hundreds of investors making millions of dollars by just buying and selling NFTs.

While NFTs are the latest sensation around crypto circles, ICOs have gotten the same attention a couple of years back.

The Wild World of ICOs

Not everyone can have sufficient capital to invest in popular cryptocurrencies such as Ethereum and Bitcoin. If you are not satisfied with the returns cryptocurrencies are giving, then you could try out some of the ICOs that are live at present. Before talking about ICOs let us inform you that they are very risky and can make you lose all of your capital. However, if you invest in a genuine ICO and if the company succeeds well, then your investment will give you high returns.

What Is an Initial Coin Offering (ICO)?

Initial coin offerings are similar to the stock market's initial public offerings. An IPO is a process by which a company that becomes publicly traded sells stocks to both private and retail investors as it enters the market. A similar process happens in the cryptocurrency market when developers want to create a new coin.

Cryptocurrency startups and established companies who need capital for new projects started to use the same concept to collect the capital necessary using initial coin offerings. However, we call this process wild because out of the many ICOs that have launched, only 20 percent have become successful. Many of them failed or were abandoned midway. Many others turned out to be scams put together to generate some quick money.

How Can Companies or Individuals Create an ICO?

The concept is pretty simple. You need to create a whitepaper that explains all the details of your project as well as the cost and timeline for completion. You can post the whitepaper along with your website or other details to a community forum. If people like your project's idea, they will send you money either in Bitcoin or in regular fiat currency.

In return, you send your ICO's supporters baby coins, which initially have no value. If the startup becomes a success, then the value of those coins will increase exponentially, and supporters can net huge profits.

Why Are ICOs Essential?

Normally, tech innovation mostly happens because someone has a wonderful idea and raises venture capital to help them bring their vision to life. This is also how other companies fund their expansions. They create IPOs, and with the generated money, they will improve the core goal of their company.

However, with cryptocurrencies, there are no regulations, and it is challenging to fund startups that are closely related to cryptocurrency. This dilemma has been addressed by ICOs, and indeed they have produced many fantastic blockchain platforms and decentralized applications that have the potential to change the world.

Initial coin offerings are essential because to create a decentralized economy, new projects and platforms must emerge. It is not only a good gesture or a risky investment, but it is also helping fellow crypto enthusiasts start their dream projects.

How Can I Start My Own ICO?

To start any ICO, you need to have the technical skills to develop a viable project. People will have many doubts about your project, so make sure you clear those doubts and make sure people clearly understand the idea you are trying to bring to the blockchain platform.

After starting an ICO, you also may need to market it using a website or enlisting help from prominent influencers, if possible. Your main goal should be to raise as much capital as you can.

Will ICOs Ever Be Regulated?

Until 2017, ICOs ran wild, and 80% of them were of no use to regular investors. People started not to take these campaigns seriously because they were not giving any value to them in return.

However, the Securities and Exchange Commission (SEC) has said that it will be checking for scams involved in the cryptocurrency market. However, ICOs are still not regulated. Many also complain that ICO regulations also dilute the core purpose of a decentralized economy. On the other hand, China has completely banned ICOs, stating that they are very unsafe for the economy.

How to Gain Profits With ICOs as an Investor

While there are many drawbacks to ICOs, they are still good investment choices that bring huge profits. On average, the top ICOs yielded 12 times the amount investors initially paid, so ICOs are still an excellent choice for investors if you understand the risk.

Do Your Research

As an investor trying to invest in an ICO, you should have a thorough knowledge of the ICO's creator. Understanding whitepapers and all the technicalities that are involved is also essential. Look at crypto forums and the discussion that the idea has raised in the blockchain community. Also, don't forget to be practical when judging an ICO. Ideas are easy to write down, but it is hard to implement them in reality.

Understand Legal Terms

Anyone who starts an ICO needs to understand all the privacy policies and tax regulations. So, make sure that you check all these policies on the creator's official website. Reading these policies can help you understand whether they are serious about what they are doing.

3) Use Listing Websites

To help enthusiastic investors, a lot of websites that list current ICOs are available. You can check out the reviews from investors. With little more than a glance, you can spot many scams on these websites.

4) Make Sure the Funds Are Going to an Escrow Wallet

ICO funds are usually stored in an escrow wallet. This wallet makes data and transaction details available to all the investors. If any ICO's creator asks for funds to be sent to their private Bitcoin or Ethereum account, they may be trying to scam you.

Ethereum, a popular blockchain platform that is now the second most popular currency, has become what it is because of investors who supported the idea behind it by ICO. ICOs work and they will give you huge returns, but it is your job to find an ICO that is legitimate and has developers who are serious about their work and hope to change the crypto world.

Regardless of whether you are investing in an NFT or an ICO or a cryptocurrency, there is always a risk. Understanding risk and developing a risk management strategy is a must for every crypto investor.

Chapter   10:   Risk   in Cryptocurrency

For any investment practice, there is always a risk. Cryptocurrencies are highly volatile and unpredictable and have a high risk factor. It is important to understand the gravity of risk while investing in order to reduce losses and increase profits. Risk management strategies can help an investor earn profits in the long term. In addition to risks from the market, you should be wary of scams that target cryptocurrency investors.

What Is a Risk?

Risk applies to every financial instrument or class. If you buy an automobile, and it is involved in an accident, the asset's value will decrease drastically. Here, an accident is a risk that can affect an asset (in this case, a car). In the same way, all financial instruments such as stocks, derivatives, and cryptocurrencies are prone to risk for various reasons. For example, a shortage in semiconductor chips can be a risk factor for all computer and technology-related stocks as all of these companies depend on those chips for production.

We will now talk about some of the significant risks that cryptocurrency investors need to understand before making any decisions.

Risks for Cryptocurrency Investors

Risk Due to Experimental Phase

Right now, blockchain technology is just in an experimental phase. While the technology itself is very innovative, there are many loopholes that we may not yet understand. Blockchain platforms are all doing hard work to create decentralized applications that can change the world. However, some are still not confident that this could work in the way everyone intended it. As we proceed further, we may understand the complications and drawbacks that blockchain platforms have, and this may decrease the underlying value of your asset.

For example, what if people thought that blockchain technology was having a massive impact on climate change due to its massive energy consumption? This is why you need to keep up with crypto news to stay aware of changes and judge the future of the technology.

Manipulation Risk

While cryptocurrencies are incredibly secure and store all your transaction information in a public ledger, they still cannot prevent investors from being manipulated. The wide popularity of crypto made it a favorite target for social engineering attacks and frauds. Misinformation is also easily spread, and it may lead you to invest in cryptocurrencies that aren't innovative enough to have future value.

Most of the manipulations happening in the cryptocurrency market are based on ICOs. Many projects that crypto investors encounter are either scams or very hard to implement in the real world.

Cybersecurity Risks

Since they are based on decentralized platforms running on the Internet, it follows that almost all cryptocurrencies and their investors are vulnerable to cybersecurity risks. Hackers are developing different machine learning and AI bots to either phish or hack the users' wallet addresses. While various services are available to mitigate cybersecurity risks, it is still a factor that can cause substantial price fluctuations.

Human Error Risks

This is the most under-discussed risk factor that investors need to be aware of. If you lose either your public or private addresses, there is no way to get them back. Your cryptocurrencies will forever be stored in the blockchain without anyone able to use them. Human error can also make investors root for cryptocurrencies that are not valuable.

Technological Risks

Blockchain is evolving with time. With rising technology, new technologies will be more powerful and innovative than existing ones. These new technologies can make the ones that already exist in crypto platforms irrelevant and pointless.

This change of technology happens in every industry. For example, Amazon has slowly reduced the popularity of brick-and-mortar stores. In the same way, a new crypto coin can decrease the popularity of Bitcoin simply because the new coin is better. This is an ever-present risk.

Hard Forking Risks

Blockchain platforms are independent and are, for the most part, dependent on the investor's decision. Hard forking happens when a specific upgrade needs to be made to the inherent philosophy or structure of the blockchain.

Hard forks are messy and can divide the community because of bad decision-making by the founders of the cryptocurrency. Ethereum classic was formed this way because the community did not agree with some decisions made by the founder.

Investors need to carefully observe the upgrade proposals and how the community reacts to them to reduce risks.

Liquidity Risks

Not all cryptocurrencies have a high liquidity rate. If you invest in alternative cryptocurrencies, you need to understand the current liquidity rate of that asset. If you can't find a buyer when there is a panic in the market, then the overall value of your asset will decrease, and your returns will be reduced.

Legal Risk

You will always be prone to legal risk if you liquidate your assets into fiat currency using exchanges such as Coinbase. There is no way to tax your crypto transactions, but when you are liquidating cryptocurrencies into your bank account, you should make sure that you pay taxes. Please consult a chartered accountant if you are not aware of taxes regarding cryptocurrencies. In the next section, we will talk about risk management strategies that every investor needs to follow.

Risk Management Strategies

Every investor needs to create their own set of risk management strategies depending on the assets they have invested in. It is always better to make your own decisions while investing or trading in cryptocurrency, especially when it comes to navigating risk.

Maintain a Diversified Bag

Never invest all your money in a single cryptocurrency. Diversification can help you to reduce your losses. As cryptocurrency is mostly about supply and demand, crypto enthusiasts can avoid many risks by investing in different cryptocurrencies with good demand.

Don't Invest Until You Understand the Currency

Investors can avoid risk if they know what they are doing. Do thorough research about cryptocurrencies before investing in them. Always measure the risk factor while doing fundamental analysis for every asset.

Use Stop Losses and Take Profits

When you use either stop losses or take profits, your asset will be sold when it reaches a particular loss or gain. Using stop losses can help you avoid betting on underperforming stocks based on emotional attachment. Take profits is also beneficial, especially if you are a day trader.

Use Both Technical and Fundamental Analysis

It is true that technical and fundamental analysis are very different and use different philosophies. However, to be successful and make profits, you need to understand both these concepts and should use them in tandem in your trades.

Understand the Risk-Reward Ratio

The risk-reward ratio helps you understand before the trade how much you are willing to lose and hope to gain. When you understand the risk-reward ratio, you will be judging the price fluctuations based entirely on your expectations. Both greed and panic reduce your profits over a long time.

Know When to Exit

In Cryptocurrencies, entrance is always easy, and exit is always complicated. To be consistent with your profits, you need to know when to exit and dump the coins.

Always Have a Plan

Planning is essential, especially for an investor. Plan strategies for each of the cryptocurrencies that you have invested in. Always have a plan but improvise when there is high volatility in the market.

Keep Educating Yourself

Always keep learning new things about your investments. Make conjectures about the future and check out any new decentralized apps that come out. Be passionate about what you are doing and network with other crypto traders. Constantly learn from webinars, conferences, and books. All your investment strategies will be dependent on the knowledge you are consuming.

Use Position Sizing

Position sizing is crucial if you are a day or swing trader. With position sizing, you will be restricted to trading only 2% of your capital for one trade. This strategy will not only minimize risks but will also help you to make immediate counter decisions if anything goes wrong.

10) Analyze and Assess

To reduce risks further, always analyze and assess both your successful and unsuccessful trades. Make a note of them and treat them as case studies.

Use Advanced Software

All cryptocurrencies are traded on the Internet, and it is pretty easy to get crypto performance charts for your analysis. You can use advanced trading software that gives you many indicators to analyze using technical analysis. Having excellent software can help you quickly find any dumps or pumps that are happening. Investors can also estimate volatility by using these software clients. Most of this software also uses AI and machine learning algorithms to predict price changes. However, you should not depend solely on this software. Your decision should always be based on human instinct.

These strategies will help you weather the fluctuations in the cryptocurrency market, but there are other risks traders should be wary of, like scams.

Cryptocurrency Scams

The value of cryptocurrencies has risen exponentially and without a doubt, the rise in these prices made many scammers turn their attention to cryptocurrency. The Bitcoin phenomenon and the coin's success is mainly due to its anonymity. Unfortunately, this anonymity also allows hackers and con artists to steal.

Ponzi Scheme Scams

These are some of the most common scams that people get lured into.

A Ponzi Scheme is an elaborate scam in which investors are promised guaranteed returns. Cryptocurrency investors are often dragged into these Ponzi schemes thanks to the currencies' decentralization and anonymity. Never believe schemes that guarantee profits. In any investment, there is no guarantee of profits.

Ponzi schemes work so well because they exploit investors' trust that people get drawn into these schemes by the trust. When a trusted authority says that a scheme works well, people will join it without a second thought. Ponzi schemes first manipulate people and then will encourage them to manipulate others.

Fake Exchange Scams

People just beginning with any cryptocurrency need to buy them using fiat currency. However, there have been a few scams in which the exchanges themselves are fake. South Korea has seen a big scam with a fake exchange. Make sure that you are investing in popular exchanges which have built trust with their customers.

Regular Scams

Scammers and crackers are still using old techniques such as the Nigerian e-mail scam to manipulate people's emotions and get the victims to send money in Bitcoins. To avoid these types of schemes, always check any suspicious e-mails with anti-spam software.

Pump and Dump Scams

These scams have existed for a long time, and they are not exclusive to cryptocurrency markets. However, pump and dump scams are a market manipulation technique that people fall prey to. Unscrupulous investors use these tactics because the victims' combined pump can increase the overall capitalization of the cryptocurrency.

To pump the cryptocurrency, the scammers make false claims to lure other investors into buying a cryptocurrency to increase the currency's price. When the scammer is satisfied with the price, they will immediately dump these coins, which causes the asset's overall price to decline.

To not be affected by these scams, make sure that you do complete research about penny cryptos before investing in them. Also, because of blockchain transparency, you can quickly check the number of users in a network. If many nodes are holding a lot of shares without any significant contribution from others, they are likely trying to game you.

Malware Scams

Many people are unknowingly installing malware that mines cryptocurrency on their computers. These malware creators are earning tens of Bitcoins by utilizing the power of thousands of computers. Install good anti-virus software not to become affected by malware scams.

Despite these risks, alternative cryptocurrencies are the future, and there is a lot of room for them to create robust and decentralized applications that can change the world.

In 2021, cryptocurrency investors are in bullish mode. There is a lot of discussion going on now in financial circles that there will be a massive change in the market capitalization of cryptocurrencies because of people's change in mindset about the concept of decentralization. People are not only intrigued by the profits but are also genuinely excited about the changes that blockchain technology may bring about.

Conclusion

Cryptocurrency is evolving day by day, and a lot of investors are rallying around the hype that is surrounding it. This book is meant to help even those who are new to crypto trading learn about the various alternatives to Bitcoin. Altcoins are everywhere, and we hope the book's information has helped you understand different alternative currencies and their advantages.

Here are some of the tips and tricks that every crypto investor needs to be aware of, regardless of the coin they are investing in. Keep reading and remember these suggestions before making an investment choice.

Tips for Cryptocurrency Investors

Always Do a Reality Check

As an investor, you must do a reality check before investing your hard-earned money in the cryptocurrency market. No investing strategy provides a guaranteed return, and you can lose all your money on a bad investment.

To do a reality check, first, understand your current financial stability and analyze your debts. It is always recommended that you become debt-free before starting to think about making any investments, especially in a highly volatile investment choice like cryptocurrency, you need to know whether you can handle any losses.

Questions for a reality check :

1. What is my current financial position?

2. Can I face the risk that comes with this asset?

3. How would a loss affect my life?

4. What is important for me right now?

5. How much do I wish to earn by investing in cryptocurrency?

Brainstorm the answers to these questions and analyze them to understand whether or not an investment is a good idea for you at this moment.

Constantly Follow News and Social Media

Financial instruments are affected by news and other important events. For example, stocks are highly influenced by political and economic news. In the same way, cryptocurrencies are also affected by news that relates to them.

A lot of countries are restricting the use of Bitcoin because of its decentralization. Whenever a country makes cryptocurrency illegal, there will be a lot of selling, and the prices of the coins will decrease. For this reason, you need to be diligent about collecting information from various outlets and crypto magazines.

Twitter is also a great place to meet investors who are supporting or cheering for your favorite blockchain. All these community resources can help you judge whether a cryptocurrency should be in your bag. Here, 'bag' refers to the word commonly used in place of portfolio by crypto investors. Following influencers such as Elon Musk is also important as they have the potential to drive the prices of a cryptocurrency up or down.

Keep Reading Peer-Reviewed Journals About Different New Blockchains

At present, there are more than 2000 different isolated blockchains in the cryptocurrency platform. All these blockchains publish whitepapers before starting them. Understanding these whitepapers and effectively judging them is an essential skill for investors.

It is also important for an investor to read peer-reviewed journals to understand the potential different blockchain platforms offer. We also recommend you follow crypto magazines to consume new information about various domains related to cryptocurrency.

Make a Trade Journal

Keeping a trade journal is essential for any investor to understand their mistakes and carefully analyze their decisions. Trade journals differ based on the person.

What should a trade journal contain?

1. Your capital and expected returns

2. When you opened your position

3. The fundamental analysis characteristics that you have considered before investing

4. Technical charts and indicators that you have considered before investing

5. Your psychological state while making this trade

6. The profit or loss that you got in return for a particular investment if you sell it

7. A score from 1-10 based on your experience with a specific trade

Maintaining a journal trade and following it carefully to learn mistakes can be a life-changing tool. You can find different templates on the Internet for a trade journal.

Don't Worry About Losses

Losses are common when investing in cryptocurrency. Don't make hasty decisions or dump a coin simply because you've had a few losses. Always remember that you are competing with thousands of investors to create an effective decentralized economy.

What to do if you are experiencing a lot of losses:

1. Take a break, and spend time with your loss.

2. Learn mental exercises such as yoga or meditation to reduce stress and help make effective decisions.

3. Realize that both losses and success are common, and you aren't the only one who is experiencing a difficult time.

4. Make a plan and don't deviate from that plan when you come back to invest and trade in the cryptocurrency market again.

Wait Patiently

Unlike publicly traded companies, cryptocurrency projects and companies developing decentralized apps take more time to complete their work because the technology is new. There are only a few experienced programmers in this domain.

This increase in timeframe can make many investors uneasy. For example, Cardano, a cryptocurrency coin that uses various advanced concepts to make cross-blockchain communication possible, did not get the attention that it deserved at first.

Even after four years, it has only reached $2 as of now. But does the investor that is holding the coins dump them and move on? No. It is still one of the popular cryptocurrencies in market capitalization right now. As an investor, you need to have the patience to wait for good to happen. Always believe in the goals and future updates for your cryptocurrencies and wait until they skyrocket.

Understand Cybersecurity and Secure Your Wallet

Even though stocks and other financial instruments are being traded with a mouse click nowadays, they are very hard to hack. All brokerage firms use extensive cybersecurity techniques to stop hackers from exploiting them either by DDOS attacks or brute-forcing.

With cryptocurrency, it is very important to have a sufficient understanding of cybersecurity because thousands of hackers are waiting to learn your public and private keys to transfer the contents of your wallet.

Some practices to not fall prey to hackers:

1. Store your passwords safely. One way to do so is by keeping them in a private password storage wallet.

2. Understand phishing and never enter your private or public keys in any online forms. Remember that no legitimate site will ask you for your sensitive information.

3. Never install any software from pirate sites. They may have Trojans installed, and these Trojans can control your computer without you knowing.

Pay Taxes

Cryptocurrencies are decentralized, and there is no way that your identity will be revealed when you exchange Bitcoin with other users in the network.

However, right now, not all platforms accept cryptocurrency as a payment medium.

This is why many Bitcoin investors liquidate their coins in need, and for this, they need to register with an online brokerage such as Coinbase to convert Bitcoin to regular currency. All these brokerage firms charge a maker and taker fee. These charges are usually high, and you will also fall under government scrutiny because of this.

However skeptical you may be of the concept of centralization, it is important to pay taxes when you liquidate your Bitcoins into real-world currency. Contact a professional chartered accountant if you are not aware of tax regulations in your country.

Always Invest in Other Financial Instruments

Cryptocurrency is the future. There is no denying that. But it is not a good move to invest all your hard-earned money in one financial strategy. Always invest in as many monetary instruments as you can to diversify your portfolio.

If you are not interested in mutual funds or derivatives, it is recommended to invest in stocks as they tend to yield huge profits on par with cryptocurrencies.

Publicly traded companies such as Apple, Tesla, Amazon, and Google are also aware of the blockchain revolution and are finding ways to incorporate blockchain technology into their services and products. It may take time, but both the cryptocurrency and stock markets will be closely linked in the future.

Control Your Emotions

Emotions play a huge role whenever there is a decision to be made. A lot of short-term price fluctuations can cause panic among investors and can then lead to selling for a loss. As an investor, you need to control your emotions and check whether the asset is valuable from all angles.

Having a favorite cryptocurrency and justifying having it even when there are significant losses is also a bad practice.

Congratulations! you have reached the end of this book and acquired some valuable knowledge about cryptocurrency and investment. Keep reading different resources, blog posts, and forums to increase knowledge about different cryptocurrency concepts and keep current. Cryptocurrency and blockchain are tremendous technologies that are going to change the world in the coming years. Keep dreaming about this exciting future!

Disclaimer:

The cryptocurrency market is very volatile and can make you lose a lot of capital if you are not sure about what you are doing. This book and the author are in no way responsible for your investment decisions. The author of the book has written this book only to spread knowledge. Please do thorough research about cryptocurrency before you invest in it.

References

Bernard Marr. *What is the difference between Bitcoin and Ripple?* (n.d.). Bernard Marr. https://bernardmarr.com/default.asp?contentID=1384

Blockchain Explained: *What is blockchain?* (n.d.). Euromoney   Learning. https://www.euromoney.com/learning/blockchain-explained/what-is-blockchain

Frankenfield, J. (2021, February 18). *Bitcoin.* Investopedia. https://www.investopedia.com/terms/b/bitcoin.asp

What is Ethereum: Understanding its features and applications. (n.d.).   Simplilearn. https://www.simplilearn.com/tutorials/blockchain-tutorial/what-is-ethereum

What is Cardano blockchain? [The most comprehensive step-by-step guide]. (2018, February   21).   Blockgeeks. https://blockgeeks.com/guides/what-is-cardano/

Wood, G. (2021, May 17). *The launch of parachains.* Medium. https://medium.com/polkadot-network/the-launch-of-parachains-78188fcf024f

Hayes, A. (n.d.). *What is Stellar?* Investopedia. Retrieved May 18, 2021, from https://www.investopedia.com/terms/s/stellar-cryptocurrency.asp

What are the risks? (n.d.). CMC Markets. https://www.cmcmarkets.com/en/learn-cryptocurrencies/what-are-the-risks

A guide to cryptocurrency fundamental analysis. (n.d.). Binance Academy. https://academy.binance.com/en/articles/a-guide-to-cryptocurrency-fundamental-analysis

8 alternatives to bitcoin you should know about. (n.d.). Money under 30. Retrieved May 18, 2021, from https://www.moneyunder30.com/alternatives-to-bitcoin

What is Tezos? The most updated deep Dive. (n.d.). Blockgeeks. https://blockgeeks.com/guides/what-is-tezos/

Borate, N. (2020, December 28). *Tether changed the way we look at cryptocurrencies.* Mint.

https://www.livemint.com/money/personal-finance/tether-changed-the-way-we-look-at-cryptocurrencies-11609085275084.html

What is Chainlink? Oracles, nodes and LINK tokens. (n.d.). Gemini. Retrieved May 25, 2021, from https://www.gemini.com/cryptopedia/what-is-chainlink-and-how-does-it-work

What is Uniswap and how does it work? (n.d.). Binance Academy. https://academy.binance.com/en/articles/what-is-uniswap-and-how-does-it-work

Wiesflecker, L. (2021, January 24). *What you need to know about The Graph (GRT).* Medium. https://medium.com/coinmonks/what-you-need-to-know-about-the-graph-grt

The complete guide to understanding EOS blockchain. (2019, July 2). LeewayHertz. https://www.leewayhertz.com/what-is-eos-blockchain/

What is Aave (AAVE)? (n.d.). Binance Academy. Retrieved May 25, 2021, from https://academy.binance.com/en/articles/what-is-aave

Algorand (ALGO) explained. (2020, November 21). Boxmining. https://boxmining.com/algorand/